To Bob & Family
Thankyou for bringing
to realization my credit
and helping me with
the refinancing. All these
thing were to bless me
and help with the books.
Thankyou so much.
Love Debbie

BANKRUPTCY

FILE WITH GOD

NOT

WITH MAN

VIKKIE VAUGHAN

NEW WRITERS' INK PUBLISHING CO., INC.
—2007—
A DIVISION OF VIKKIE VAUGHAN LITERARY
www.vikkievaughan.com

BANKRUPTCY
Published by
New Writers' Ink Publishing Co., Inc. (NWI)

All scripture quotations are from:
The Holy Bible, King James Version (KJV)
© 1963 Dakes Annotated Ref. Bible

NWI, its logos, and marks are trademarks of
New Writers' Ink Publishing Co., Inc.

Publisher: Vikkie Vaughan
Founder and C.E.O. of New Writers' Ink Publishing Co., Inc. A Division of Vikkie Vaughan Literary—www.vikkievaughan.com

Artistic Direction: Book, cover, page concept, layout, and design by Vikkie Vaughan

Graphics for Cover: Andrew Hall, owner A.M.I. Studios

Inside formatting and typesetting: Mystic Publishers

Project Production, Management, and
Editorial by: Vikkie Vaughan

Library Of Congress Cataloging in Publication Data

ISBN: 978-0-9774419-2-1

1. God 2. Faith 3. Prayer 4. Christian Living 5. Spiritual Growth

Printed in the United States of America

Other Books By Vikkie Vaughan

TRUSTING GOD
© 2006
ISBN 10: 0-9774419-7-0
ISBN 13 : 978-0-9774419-7-6

WITH THIS RING
©2007
ISBN 13: 978-0-9774419-1-4

Table of Contents

Acknowledgements

I acknowledge my Lord and Savior Jesus Christ, to whom I give all honor and glory. Thank you, Lord, for giving me dreams, and visions and for releasing your golden nuggets of divine inspiration; the unction to write this book.

I thank you, Lord, for this wonderful book; to help encourage others to step out of trusting in themselves as they begin to acknowledge trusting you in all their ways, so you can direct their paths.

Thank you for helping me to assist others on how to walk by faith and not by sight, thus reaping all the benefits of walking in greater faith, joy, peace, happiness, strength, and wisdom.

I lift my head, hands, and voice to you in praise! Rejoicing for the great work you're perfecting in my life.

I thank you for the divine revelation in filing bankruptcy with you and not with man in a court of law. I thank you for proving yourself and bringing me into complete victory.

I pray that "your glory" be manifested at all times through my ministry with the books you've given me to write for you, as they all go forth in Jesus' Name.

Dedications

I dedicate this book to all of my children: To Kimberly, who is a great little warrior, loving God so much. You have blessings untold. To Candice, who has a heart of gold and is a giver. God has a lot of work for you to do. To Bryan, my little sojourner, a very hard worker. Don't give up! God knows your heart and hears your prayers. To Anthony, my first born, who is so gifted, being very talented. I am so proud of your many, many achievements. God wants to use you mightily.

To all of my children, grandchildren, and those who are yet to come; these words I declare for your benefit as words of wisdom.

Proverbs 3: 1-9

Verse 1: "My son, forget not my law; but let thine heart keep my commandments:"

Verse 2: "For length of days, and long life, and peace, shall they add to thee."

Verse 3: "Let not mercy and truth forsake thee: bind them about thy neck; write them upon the table of thine heart:"

Verse 4: "So shalt thou find favour and good understanding in the sight of God and man."

Verse 5: "Trust in the Lord with all thine heart; and lean not unto thine own understanding."

Verse 6: "In all thy ways acknowledge him, and he shall direct thy paths."

Verse 7: "Be not wise in thine own eyes: fear the Lord, and depart from evil."

Verse 8: "It shall be health to thy navel, and marrow to thy bones."

Verse 9: "Honour the Lord with thy substance, and with the first-fruits of all thine increase:"

To my mother, Alberta, both fathers, J.D. and Jesse; my sisters Brenda and Tammie; my brothers Dewayne (in memory of) and Robert. With this explanation, I offer these pages of my life, helping all of you understand who I really am. This is the cause that was always so important to me. This is the reason why I'd have to withdraw myself at times; so please be patient with me. Nevertheless, you *are* my family and I'll *always* love you no matter what—but there were just more times than none that I had to stretch out on faith, dwelling in the secret place of the most High. Abiding under the shadow of the Almighty. I will say of the Lord, He is my refuge, my fortress: My God; in Him will I trust.

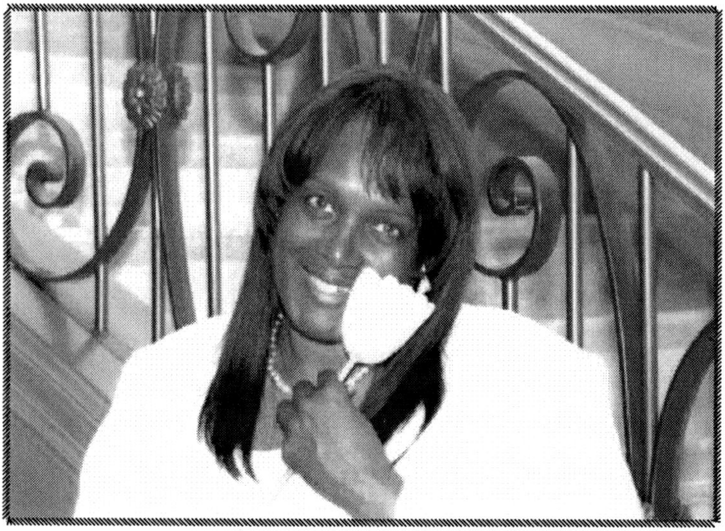

Author's Biography

I'm a native of Las Vegas, Nevada. I have four beautiful children and ten grandchildren at present. Of great importance and also one of the most exciting aspects of my life is that I'm a born-again Christian. I attend Word of Life Christian Center.

All knowledge, wisdom, and understanding that I've gained is based on my personal relationship with God, with the acceptance of His word. My perseverance, being consistent in reading, hearing, studying and properly standing on the Word has opened floodgates of miracles to me.

I've overcome many obstacles by taking hold of faith; stepping out of the boat unto the water. In being obedient, moving quickly when inclined by the Holy Spirit gives reason as to how I triumph over all my fears. Thus, I become a great achiever.

However, the most precious facet of all is how I love The Lord. It gives me great joy with honor being obedient to God's will in drawing souls to Him. In sharing the love of God as to how precious He really is, gives me great pleasure in sharing with you my heart, joy, and experiences that are all motivated by compassion.

Symbolism of the Book's Cover

My dear and cherished readers, let's take a brief moment in silence for a word of prayer.

Father, I want to acknowledge and thank you for ushering me to share with the world something that you have been doing for decades, but not many have been willing to share.

I pray that the hands that pick up this book will not be embarrassed to read it, accept it, acknowledge it, and to share it in full or in parts with others. I pray that the hearts of my readers be moistened, yet softened, to soak up as in a sponge these powerful words, wisdom, knowledge and declarations set by God with such high standards from your true and living word.

I thank you, Father, because I know without a shadow of a doubt that people throughout the nation shall be delivered, and will finally have that financial freedom that they seek and desire for a clear pathway to be debt free and abundantly prosperous, with peace, joy, and happiness along the way. Amen.

BANKRUPT: Legally declared unable to pay one's debts because of the lack of money, and in turn, having one's remaining property administered by, or divided among one's creditors. Completely, or in part of being without money (liquid assets); financially ruined.

ELECTROCARDIOGRAM: The curve traced by an electrocardiograph for the studying in the rhythm of one's heart and diagnosing its disease.

The description in part used here is for the diagnosing of a disease called **bankruptcy** of one's wallet. However, as one begins to get back on track, you can begin to breathe easy and gain control of your life once again; you're stabalized with a good arrythmia.

FLATLINE: The activity in the electrocardiograph has ceased. In respect to the cover, based on our lives, the noose has tightened around our wallet thus affecting our lives and we begin to lose activity. We can't do anything. Deprivation has become our best friend. There is nothing left. We can't go forward, and we can't go backward. When going through bankruptcy, we become lifeless and begin to surrender as we conclude. Once there is flatline, we have relinquished and ceased.

GRID: A framework of crisscrossed bars, the struggles that weigh you down and keep you from achieving those new heights and new levels. It is any pattern or network of crossing lines or elements, especially when arranged in a parallel set. **"Gridlocked"** (you've hit rock bottom).

NOOSE: A loop formed in a rope by means of a slipknot so that it binds tighter as the rope is pulled or tugged. It could be a snare or a trap. Something that is very real that **restricts** your freedom.

STAIRS: Represent new heights and new levels within the grid.

WALLET: A small flat case for holding paper money, coins, etc.

X: The letter X has a lot of different meanings, and connotations. *X marks the spot where the treasure is buried.* The X can also be used to mark out something not to be used anymore.

1) The connotation used here in bankruptcy means: I filed bankruptcy with God.

2) I decided not to use man in the court of law.

3) Therefore, "I found my treasure in God" and not in man!

THOUGHT FOR TODAY

HAVE YOU CONSIDERED FILING

BANKRUPTCY

WITH GOD

AND

NOT WITH MAN

THROUGH A COURT OF LAW

?

A BREAKTHROUGH IN YOUR FINANCIAL

FREEDOM

A GUIDE ON HOW TO BE DEBT FREE

Introduction

Are you being haunted by debt, lack, and deprivation? Are you having trouble trying to figure out where, or who, or how to turn to anyone?

Are you sick and tired of being tired, with lack on your back lurking everywhere you turn, from the North, South, East, and West?

Are you drooping from that black cloud of gloom that's been hanging over you and your home, torturing your mental state, and robbing you of every bit of your joy, and all of your peace?

Are you in despair, having one or two feet in the pit of doom with no immediate help or way out?

Are you disgusted with having to sit down month after month going over all of your bills trying to figure out who will get paid this month or the next?

Are you weary with drawing straws, exhausted with the tossing of coins, drained with the shuffling around, or putting in a bag each bill to then close your eyes and pull the bill for the month to get paid?

Are you barely getting by with very little money, if any at all, completely feeling anxious, with sleepless nights regarding your financial status?

Are you collapsing with the bothersome calls that embarrass you and upset you even more, bringing you to the brink of tears, perhaps a smoke, pills, or even a drink?

Are you constantly being choked out by the weeds and the deadly infestation that eat at the crops in your field? Are you bombarded and harassed day in and day out?

Are you stressed and depressed, feeling as though you should contact an attorney to declare yourself unable to pay your debts because of lack, and the costly amounts of your financial obligations?

Are you bankrupt and now in a financially ruined state?

Are things so bad that you have hit rock bottom and there is a possible need for the courts to abide over, orchestrate, administer, or possibly divide your remaining property among your creditors to pay your bills? Has it actually gone that far?

If any of these scenarios fit you and it sounds like your intense situation, more or less, then this book is definitely for you. The A's have it and I would like to share with you, my readers, my downfall, my pit, and the ruin that I came to know.

I would like to also share with you the awesome turn around in my life because of the faithfulness in God and all of His promises that ultimately led to the triumph of my success, and the victories won.

I waged a war, and the battle was won toward being bankrupt by "FILING BANKRUPTCY WITH GOD" and "NOT WITH MAN THROUGH A COURT OF LAW." I call it my ***sweet, sweet victory!***

Author's Preface

On January 8, 2001, at approximately 8:50 a.m., I sustained a severe injury as a result of slipping and falling at work. I ruptured my tailbone, herniated discs in my back, tore ligaments while rupturing the cartilage in both knees. In addition, damage occurred to my neck, shoulder, arm, and hand, including breaking a finger. The events of that day proved to be one of the most *unbelievable* turning points of my life.

After being taken to the emergency room, I was forced to go back to work, continuing to work daily against my will, combined with all the pain. I say my will, because I was told that if I left, or called in sick without *their* doctor's notification, I could be terminated. Therefore, I was afraid of losing my job.

My supervisor also informed me that I could not take any prescribed medication for pain during work, only over-the-counter medications such as aspirin. I never felt so low, being helpless, overtaken with exhaustion. My spirit was broken, just like that of a wild animal in captivity. I was absolutely ready to give up!

However, God the Father stepped in, blessing me with a new set of doctors who took over my care. They urged my supervisor to place me on a medical leave-of-absence after approximately four months of agony, allowing me to go forward with the surgery needed from my accident related injuries. God spoke to my spirit, advising me that He did not want me to be idle during this time. Then what was I suppose to do? The Lord gave me in detail: information, direction, along with instructions to do something very special in order to rebuild my spirits, which I've been doing ever since. I began to go through a series of events with challenges that completely changed my life.

God's master plan was so unique, needless to say, incredible, that it *restored* my life! He said... "You are a writer and I want you to write books for me." Now over the years that I've been writing letters to God, I increased in that ability, turning those letters into short manuscripts.

Some may query as to what they were all about. They consisted of in-depth conversation regarding my personal relationship with Him. I expressed all my failures, weaknesses, the sorrowfulness, my cry for help, etc. Those times that I spent with the Lord, took me to a place (my secret closet) where I can find rest, refuge, peace, joy, and happiness, telling God *everything*. This was my way of praying daily, also making my requests known, and expressing my feelings toward Him with thanksgiving, praise, and song. I've found and confirmed along the way that these things were always in preparation for my future. Oh, how great thou art!

Immediately, the Lord came to me in dreams, and gave me visions to prepare the way for me to do His work. God showed me exactly what I needed to do, showing me how to do it. I've been very excited ever since. Most of all I've been obedient, because I know in my heart this is where it all begins—*being obedient to God.*

I must admit that the enemy has been very busy setting up roadblocks in every direction, but I can't let that stop me. I have a mission, a divine desire to **please** the Lord. My experience has taught me that you do "not" play around with God. When He asks you to do something, you'd better move right at that moment, continuing until it is done.

Therefore, I know this is the beginning of something great! It puts me closer to my heart's desire, which is my calling: "to draw souls for Christ," combined with the *gift of giving*. My soul's desire is to retire from my job, going out in the field to work. I'd like to feed and help God's people, the homeless, or less fortunate. With confirmation that through my obedience, I hold the key to my success; that is the promise of God.

Chapter I

My War Against Bankruptcy

Now I would like to give you more of an in-depth insight as to how I continued my quest in *filing bankruptcy with God and not with man.* I filled out all of the paperwork and handed it over to God.

What I mean by this is that I gave that entire situation to God, telling him that the circumstances surrounding me were just too big for me and that I needed Him desperately; His help and His guidance.

When I turned over all of my bills fully to Christ, along with my long list of prayer requests, there wasn't any mention of payment or fee. All that God requested of me was to completely trust in Him and continue with the paying of my tithes. God also wanted me to watch Him prove Himself to me based on the divine revelation of His word.

God proved Himself very strong without faltering. He proved Himself to be more than I could have ever imagined or understood through His word. God proved His love to me over and over again, time after time.

After the filing of my partition, I decided to take drastic measures of faith.

Now listen very carefully to what I am saying.

This is my testimony to what I did as my leap of faith. I didn't have enough to pay my bills because I had hit rock bottom after losing my job.

When I discuss the term rock bottom, I mean nothing was left. The last big portion of money that I had in my hands; I recall sitting on my bed with an envelope of cash to calculate and add in the paying of my bills, was misplaced in a twinkling of an eye. To this very day, some years later, I have yet to find that envelope. It is long gone.

After that major catastrophe happened to me, I was done! This was the end of the road where I had to get off. This was the very last straw. That was the very last of any money that I had since I lost my job. As awful as it may sound, I do remember holding on very tight to this money, afraid to let go and tithe any of it or sow any of it into the kingdom of heaven because it was all I had. Besides, it wasn't quite enough for all of the bills that I had, or enough for food or gas either, so therefore I didn't pay anything at all.

I got mad with the devil, and I got busy with the Lord. I knew if anyone could help me, it would surely be the Lord. I asked God for forgiveness, picked myself up, dusted myself off, and I began a new thing. I began to sow seeds from every bit of money that came in contact with my hands, no matter how great and no matter how small, including pennies that I would find.

Through my faithfulness, the Lord blessed me with a new job. I continued in this manner and as some would say, maybe to an extreme, but I began to tithe my paychecks, keeping out just enough for a little food and gas to make it to church and back to work once again and this worked for me.

After some time, money began to come from different directions as I will mention within the book. Sometime thereafter is when I had another big test and that was with my injury. I was off from work on disability and as you know, that pay does not meet your needs.

After trusting God for such a long period of time, building a strong foundation, and a personal relationship while watching Him manifest Himself to me, I was afraid to go backward. How could I? So I continued taking God's money right off the top of my disability and all of the bills continued to get paid.

I began to get in a terrible slump though from the pain and agony of the injury. I became so weak, tired, and lifeless. I didn't want to be here any longer. However, the Lord used my books that He ordained me to write to restore my life and get me back on track again. Through my obedience, the gifts of God continued to manifest themselves.

Through the writing of my first book, I received my healing and completed the book. Through my obedience, and the paying of my tithes, the Lord laid on my heart that it was time to move out of my home into a new one, as this was one of my prayer requests that I had mentioned earlier.

Throughout this time of hearing from the Lord, I began to smell the scent of fresh paint, but the enemy wanted me to hesitate as I began thinking about my credit. I thought, who in his right mind would give me a brand new home? I was single, divorced, and not quite in the favorable bracket that would warrant such a move.

I called up a realtor who advised me of a banker to see. The young lady advised me of only two of the many items on my credit report that I needed to take care of upon the sale of my home. The very next day the bank called to give me the news regarding the application of the loan.

Can you believe that the loan was approved for an astronomical amount of money for the purchase of a new home? She had given me a copy of my credit report the previous night and I was flabbergasted as to all of the junk that was on my credit report. It was incredible. The report was a few pages thick without a clear line peeking through anywhere!

I couldn't believe that I was approved by any bank of such high standards after the review of my records. This proved to me one thing; that God was in control. When God is orchestrating all the moves in your life, there is nothing that man can do to withhold the blessings of God from you. There will be pure favor from God and man. This is the promise of God.

Once I turned everything over to God, I put forth my best effort to live the life that his word commanded. I paid my tithes, I trusted in Him. My Lord and Savoir began to show me the true meaning of His promises.

The Lord worked it out from the interest rate to the close of escrow. The Lord blessed me with a low five percent interest on my home, which dropped within a matter of a few weeks and went immediately back up again after I locked in the rate.

The realtor advised me to go with the builder because the loan carried incentives. I did and the lender didn't even bother to ask me to pay off anything. I did anyway and I kept my receipts for two years, promising myself to mail in copies to the creditors. I went back to the builder just a few weeks ago to discuss business regarding refinancing my home and asked if he would run my credit.

Well, the same young man who helped me with this home was helping now. "Oh Vikkie, your credit is wonderful and your score is at an all-time high. Look at this; it is white as snow." Just imagine that! Now how do you think that came about? Praise God; hallelujah and glory, to God's Holy name.

He stated there was one thing on the report for five hundred dollars; did I know who it might be? I advised him no, but I was willing to pay it if I owed it. He advised me to give him a few days to check it out and he would get back to me.

I called a few days later and this is what he had to say, "Vikkie, that charge does not belong to you." I said, "What? Praise God!" Then I asked how could I get it taken off of my credit records. He said not to worry that he had already taken care of it and my credit score was elevated even higher.

Now I'd like to make mention that this young man is a Christian also, so to me this was a divine situation for both of us. First of all, he was blown away because he couldn't really understand how my home or my vehicle (which was just paid off a few weeks prior) and immediate bills were all getting paid and on time, I might add, when my paychecks didn't warrant such acts.

What is even more ironic is that he couldn't quite fathom how I could maintain all of my medical, health, dental, and life insurances, IRAs, stocks, and a 401k. He asked me how could I do this. I simply stated to him with no fancy words or terms, "The Lord!"

He just continued saying over and over again

how they loved me over there, and I was able to refinance with my choice out of the best top eight scenarios. I stepped out on faith for the Lord for my ministry for Him (the books). The additional amount that I would pay out each month was going to come from a portion of the additional money I now had, since paying off of my vehicle.

However, God had something else in mind. Within a matter of days, I was informed of a new position on my job that I would be in training for. That additional pay, and the raise that I received a few weeks prior would meet that need that I just discussed prior and make the difference.

Look at God; isn't He incredible? I love Him so much. Now, upon receiving my blessing based on God's instruction and my obedience, I took the Lord's right off the top! God also instructed me to sow additional seeds in other ministries and in the lives of others as well.

What was so astonishing was that the list was so long, but I could hear Him say: "*Do not be afraid to let go,*" and everywhere I turned there was something advising me of that instruction. I know it was my test, so as God instructed me through this entire process, I was obedient with much excitement and gladness in my heart to all of His instructions regarding this venture. Praise God!

Through all of this, the Lord also showed me how to put together a very attractive portfolio package. Believe it or not, He just showed me (this very second) that he is setting me up and preparing the way for me in my ministry. God reassures me with these verses:

Psalms 84: 11-12: "For the Lord God is a sun and shield: the Lord will give grace and glory: no good *thing* will he withhold from them that walk uprightly." **Verse 12:** "O Lord of hosts, blessed *is* the man that trusteth in thee."

Deuteronomy 28: 12: "The Lord shall open unto thee his good treasure, the heaven to give the rain unto thy land in his season, and to bless all the work of thine hand: and thou shalt lend unto many nations, and thou shalt not borrow."

Now, this is why the Lord urged me to do this book on Bankruptcy at this given moment. My bankruptcy has been completed and closed within the last few days. The Lord had to actually bring it back to my attention because I had completely turned it over to Him and had forgotten all about it.

I have none of the usual effects, scars, or marks from the grief that bankruptcy can sometimes bring upon you, your family, and your credit. My ultimate goal is to be **DEBT FREE** and I can truly say that I am on my way! My credit has been completely restored, my debt has remained at a minimum for the past several years and all that I presently owe anyone is for my home, and that is my next big venture and leap of faith with the Lord. I know that it is possible! Therefore, I am thanking the Lord right now because it is already done! Since this book is based on experience and on outcome, God wanted me to share my extraordinary venture and complete victory in Him with you. If you will allow me, I would like to help, guide, and assist you when all else have failed.

Chapter II

Circumstances That Can Lead To Bankruptcy

Many circumstances can lead you to bankruptcy and financial deficit. The loss of one's job, sickness or death of a spouse, child, or a loved one. Possibly getting a divorce, child support payments, combined with the arrears that are not coming on a regular basis to help meet some of your needs. Or maybe, you're not receiving anything at all. Perhaps decisions are tied up in a court of law.

What may also be an important factor, on the flip side of the coin, leading you into financial deficit would be having to pay out an over abundance of child support, combined with possible arrears. In some cases, you might have barely enough left over to make it to your next paycheck. Therefore, if you've committed to new responsibilities, because you've just gotten married, or remarried, this could place a new burden on you. This could also cause a hardship for your new spouse and children, trying to meet the needs of two households. It can bring about stress due to worrying that may or most likely will bring about disruption within your new family.

Other associated circumstances could include: unexpected injuries of any kind that would prevent you from working and taking care of yourself and others who are dependent on you; unpredictable medical expense; an unexpected tragedy; IRS garnishment and seizures; credit card debt, bank overdraft debt, and school debt. Unforeseen circumstances could occur at any given time. You should also be aware of the infamous debt that most of us have probably incurred at one time or another: borrowing (i.e., robbing Peter to pay Paul.)

These are just a few prime examples of circumstances that could happen to lead you into financial deficit or even bankruptcy. Even if you feel that you're prepared, no one is really ready for events that seem to catch you by surprise, sending you hurtling over the edge.

Before any of these occurrences take place in your life, you may have an inner feeling of preparedness, but you cannot depend on that feeling. You cannot trust in yourself, in others, or in your finances; you must trust God! Some of these circumstances, no matter how well established you may have become over the years, can still take a drastic turn in an unfavorable direction. Meanwhile, these things can be very devastating, affecting not only you, but the lives of your family members as well.

Now before things begin to spiral downward your checking account is carrying more than a substantial amount. Your savings account balance (your stash) is at an all-time high. It's doing well with the return of dividends, along with your stock, with a few IRA accounts. The bills are all paid. The family is doing great. There's no sickness. There's joy, peace, happiness, and most of all, contentment. The head of the household is relaxed, enjoying the moment, feeling that everything is all right at this time.

It reminds me of a shepherd with his or her flock. When all is well, he is finally at rest. Of course, there's nothing wrong with that either. It gives him a wonderful sense of accomplishment. Now, although things might be going quite well, if he or she is a good shepherd, he/she will always keep an eye open, alert at all times, being prepared for any signs of trouble or danger.

Continuous prayer may be a good place to start. You never know when or where disaster is going to strike, or what's beyond what you can actually see, hear, or feel. This means you must stay prayerful, never ceasing. Never lose sight, getting too comfortable. At all times you have to stay prepared, ready for the next test that God may have. These tests are not intended to mistreat or harm you in any way.

They're only there to elevate you for your growth. There is always the possibility of failing the test, thus spiraling rapidly downward. This could mean that you would have to repeat the same test in one way or another.

However, in God's eyes, it is the endurance. Not giving up is of importance to God. He looks at your heart, and remember that He is only a prayer away. You must keep in mind that when you're living for the Lord, at some point during that time you will be under the attack of the enemy because it's his job to cause problems. However, you can declare with confidence, when something gets in the way of the mission you're on for God, when you're sincere and really mean business, you call or cry out to God about it, He will remove that obstacle, or take you completely out of that situation. I'm a living witness and know this for a fact! Try God to see. He will make your yoke easier and lighten your burden when you give it all to Him.

Stay prepared for the Lord at all times. No matter what it is He wants you to do, no matter how bad it gets, just obey! You could never be any more prepared without God. The only way to have the best outcome is to have the Lord on your side. Trust in the Lord because He will never leave or forsake you.

When your life takes a drastic turn because of the unexpected or when you're in a complicated situation, don't panic. Don't make a bad decision by turning your back on God saying that it's all His fault, because it's not. We never stop to analyze what has happened in our lives. We just run with the notion that God is behind everything that is bad.

Some of us curse God. We disrespect Him and His holy name. We talk to Him in any manner, unkind, with tone and bad attitude. It's absolutely awful! When you get angry, speak with tone, attitude, and authority to the devil. That's who's attacking you, not God. He loves you more than words could ever say. Remember, He gave His only son to die for you. That should mean something!

Once you've come to terms with this silly notion, realize that God is in your corner and get a grip on yourself. Go back to the source and ask for forgiveness. Cry out in prayer, allowing God to see you through the crisis. If you don't, your whole world of prosperity, good health, wealth, joy, peace, and happiness will be turned upside down in an instant. It can be here today and gone tomorrow.

You can expect the devil to try and turn things not only upside down, but inside out as well. He's sly, slick, yet very cunning, knowing those times when he is so good at it. Tell me, why would he change his strategy now in midstream? He's tried to be successful with his mess upon the earth since the beginning of time.

However, God surpasses all of these things. He is so much better at what He does. It's always a perfect display. Nothing and no one can put asunder the things of Christ. Never…ever, not anything that He purposes to do. Let's take a look at **Deuteronomy 8: 2:** "And thou shalt remember all the way which the Lord thy God led thee these forty years in the wilderness, to humble thee, *and* to prove thee, to know what *was* in thine heart, whether thou wouldest keep his commandments, or no."

During the course of any of these situations, you might have been, or may be experiencing several different mixed emotions about what has occurred.

When all has been said and done, one thing that may stay in the back of your mind is how you're going to make it through this. Your answer is the Lord. Do not forget that! He will always see you through. Just let Him humble you, proving what's in your heart; hopefully it is the love that you have for Him.

Show Him that just because you're going through difficult times, you won't turn your back on Him or His word. Prove to God that you believe He is who He says He is and what He stands for.

Know that somewhere out there in this vast world, there is someone who has come to the same fork in the road where you now find yourself. It happens to the best of us and you are not alone.

Chapter III

Demanding Great Sacrifices

Let's take a look at your nest egg before it all starts to dwindle away. You've been saving for more pleasant circumstances, other than the ones that have occurred, as previously mentioned. We seem to feel a little more confident when we know that there is something held over, for what some may call a rainy day. We feel comfortable, very safe in having our little stash. The very time we begin to feel a little too confident in our resources instead of God, that's when the rug is pulled right out from under us. It's often regarded as a wake-up call.

There are times in our lives when we take our eyes off of God. He's the one who gives us power to get wealth. We begin to feel that we *under our own power and might* have done all the work, feeling very confident in our achievements, thinking, "with no help from God." This is by far the Wrong Answer! It is so untrue! This is where we begin to trust in our resources rather than the nature of those resources.

Meanwhile, the funds are readily available and on hand from your nest egg. God is now petitioning you for the work of His kingdom by way of some of those funds. However, at the time of the request you decided not to obey, not to do what

God wanted you to do. For whatever the reasons might have been, you didn't obey at the right time; *your season*.

In the meantime, something comes up, possibly involving all that you have, all that you've been holding onto so tightly. What do you do now, when you haven't had a personal experience with God surrounding these types of circumstances? You may falter if you're continually trusting in yourself, others, or your finances. (Please read "*TRUSTING GOD*?" by Vikkie Vaughan.) One answer to the situation regarding your finances is to get additional help, maybe another job.

In some cases this may not always work. By the time something comes through, you're faced with the question, "Should I use the funds to help my situation, or do I give them to the Lord for which He petitioned me for in the first place?"

Trusting in the Lord is your first answer. No questions, no doubts, no second thoughts. This is the correct answer. Now maybe by this time, a job of some kind has come through for you. You are working very hard, being underpaid. You're not receiving enough money to do anything. It's not working out for you and nothing is coming together. Are you familiar with this scenario?

It takes every bit of what you're making, plus more, to get where you need to go, doing what you need to do. Guess what? This is still not remotely close to what you're used to having to live on. Your worth alone, with all the extensive education you have, now leaves you feeling worthless. These are the times when you're worth much more than what you're getting. However, it's the only thing available at this time. It's not quite making ends meet, or coming close to contributing to the type of lifestyle that you've become so accustomed too.

Then someone in your household might have the audacity to say, "I don't want to eat this," or "I don't like that." Can you relate? I'm sure some of you can. During this low peak in your life the actions of others are beginning to really irritate you, touching your heart, and making you sad all at the same time. Reality is beginning to set in. You're not very happy about what you're feeling, hearing, or seeing as you take another look around you.

As you're riding along thinking about what has just occurred, you come across homeless families living on the streets; people are sleeping on the sidewalks. There are some who only need spare change just to get something to eat. Meanwhile, there are others around you who just do not appreciate the little things that would mean so much to someone who is less fortunate.

At this time, perhaps some of your family members are not being very understanding; they're being unreasonable, there seems to be no one around who is offering a word of encouragement to you, while others refuse to join in family prayer regarding your needs and the situation. All of these things give you a feeling that there's something wrong with this picture.

This lesson is not to convict or to condemn anyone. It makes you aware of the fact that because things have changed you can't be so tight-fisted, trying to hold on to every little thing for yourself. You have to continue to pray fervently, moving when God tells you to move. This could mean giving so that God can multiply and give back, helping you through this ordeal.

At this point, it's getting very hard to make it financially while keeping some of the things you've purchased on which you are making payments. For that matter, you may be feeling compelled to start selling some of those things you own, trying to make extra money. Days have turned into weeks, and weeks into months with you needing some source of additional income that is going to see you through.

Unemployment compensation will not put you back on course. If you've lost your job, it will cover a very small portion. It will not take care of you and your family. Again, I ask you, "What will you do?" Before any of these things began to happen, God was speaking to your heart, asking you to give a portion of your nest egg as an act of faith along with obedience. This was your test. At the time the Lord asked you to give this portion you were probably in full agreement because you had it to give. Maybe more than what God was even asking of you.

It would have been easier if you had moved right then. However, you didn't move quite rapidly enough when everything seemed to be going well. Why? There were no problems at that time. Everything seemed to be great for you. You were excited, and ready to obey. You couldn't wait to do what the Lord had asked you to do, because you knew it would make your Father in heaven very happy. You were absolutely elated before any of these events began to take place.

Have you been through this before, or are you going through this now? Has everything fallen apart, bringing you to this fork in the road, this particular test? Although you haven't used all of the funds in your nest egg, it looks as though things aren't getting any better, so you begin to fear the unknown. The amount the Lord asked you to give prior to the onset of these circumstances wasn't so bad. Now you view it as quite a lot. I hear you saying, "Maybe I can do this at a later date?" No, you can't!

I know you're feeling like you can't let anything go. You feel like your family is on the verge of falling apart. You have that desperate need. Things around your household are going undone. You begin to make up all kinds of excuses. You begin to rationalize about the situation. When that doesn't work, fear, panic, doubt, and guilt all seem to set in. You need some sort of justification for holding on to those funds. You feel that they are the very essence of your being, as if it's the only thing you have left to hold on to. It makes you feel as though you still have a little something you can cling to. It feels tangible, real, something you can actually see.

Now, tell me why is it that when things start to fall apart all around us we need to see things with our own eyes to know that it is reality? We also need to touch things with our hands to feel confident that they're real. Let's take some time out to really think about this. Our acceptance of Christ is all based on faith; you've never physically seen Him or touched Him. During this time you've allowed your faith to soar. Why can't we have that same faith during these times; why change now! Have you ever thought about that before?

It is God, and only God. Trust in the Lord. If you've never gotten out of your boat to walk on the water before, believing that you could with Jesus, then this is definitely the time to get out of the boat and do so. Now, if you didn't obey you went against God's wishes regarding what he petitioned you to do earlier.

You vowed to do it, but you didn't. Due to the lack of knowledge, or whatever the case may have been, you were probably experiencing a feeling of condemnation. If so, with all sincerity, come into repentance while you're in the midst of not passing your test.

Back to the small words, 'later date.' In essence, it has more of a contrite meaning. A much larger word 'delay' or maybe the word 'rebellion' has greater significance. Being disobedient for that moment could possibly be too late for God's season of blessings for you, which is in His timing. It makes your test null and void. This is actually the purpose of the test, to see if you'll obey in a timely manner upon God's request.

A good example to help you understand is that God's blessing is like a very, very big wave or a tide. You have to be prepared to catch it at the right time so you can get on, riding it as an experienced surfer does. If the surfer catches it at just the right time, he rides the wave to its highest peak. That has to be such an exhilarating rush, with an awesome feeling of achievement.

If he misses it, though, the force of that same wave forces him to fall down! It traps him under the water! The waves wash right over him with great force and speed! This tremendous power weighs him down! Being tossed to and fro, capsized like a boat! He's finally subdued. The final determination of the results is that he's been badly hurt by the fierce beating of that pounding wave.

Wait a minute—he's moving, he's getting up. He seems to be okay, yet something is not right.

What could it be? Do any of these scenarios seem like the onset to the repercussion of things that follow after disobedience?

What I'm saying to you is get on the road of obedience. Meaning right then and right there, when God tells you to do something. Then get ready to ride the peak of that wave or tide right up to an awesome explosion into the blessings of God! If you're not, it means you're being disobedient.

This means you're not only capsized but hurled into the midst of hurt, pain, and a lot of anguish! An aftermath of devastating results because your emotional feelings, as well as your heart, got involved. They get battered, thus leaving your state of mind shattered for a period of time.

Let's explore a little more regarding the surfer. You might be wondering what else could have been wrong. In paying close attention to him, there was a sadness about him. His pride seemed to have been crushed. Then there was this look in his eyes. You know the look you're so familiar with, that ominous look of disgust and despair, as well as so much disappointment.

The frown on his face, the verbal sighs muttered or spoken aloud were the usual signs of disgust. However, his only focus was on the timing of catching that wave at the right time; nothing else!

Some of the most valuable lessons to be learned here are: obedience, timing, and being persistent when you need to if you should miss the right moment. Even though the surfer misses the wave, with certainty, he will get up brushing himself off. He continues with persistence to try over again until he gets it right. He's trusting in his confidence that if he does what he's supposed to do at just the right time, he will succeed.

Trusting God? Or trusting in self, others, or finances? How would this type of action prove to God that you're trusting in Him? It would prove that you're at least trying, giving it all you have because of who or what you love. Maybe you're not succeeding right now, but your willingness to continue trying to be successful is what counts.

On to the next step. When your pockets are filled to overflowing and there isn't a need, this is called excess; an abundant status. What is the need for this type of test? Its purpose is usually the testing of faith and your obedience, along with the love for God. There are times that are less difficult and require very little or no effort to give, but it's much easier when there's excess and you don't feel the pinch or the inconvenience of giving. However, there are times when you need to stretch beyond what you feel is your limit.

You need to go beyond where you're used to going, but never dreamed of or even dared to go before. So step out! See what God will do for you because this is how we build our faith; increasing the returns on our dividends. It doesn't matter what you may be going through, or how hard your tests are if you're not obedient to the first portion of the test. The rest of the test, being problem related issues brought on by your disobedience, will increasingly begin to come at every turn. One explanation is in comparison to the labor when birthing a child.

Ask anyone who has experienced childbirth, or perhaps who has been by the side of someone to support them during intervals of labor. From looking on or through experience, someone can confirm that at some point, there is hardly a chance to relax, breath, or regain your composure before there is another contraction. Then seconds later there's another, then another. The conclusion drawn is in comparison to your constant struggle—a great travail. These results have similar characteristics when you're not being humble. You're proving to God what's near and dear to your heart. So, this could be a prime example of the scripture given to you before from **Deuteronomy 8:2.**

I know some of you might be asking me how I would know? Have you gone through any of this? The answer is yes! I've experienced everything that I've written within these pages. Therefore, when others tell me of their experiences whether they've been a sweet success or failure, I'm always interested in knowing the choices that were made, and the reason why. Of course you always want to make the right decision, but sometimes you don't. Therefore, it makes me feel the need to reach out, helping others overcome their obstacles, giving support; with yet another confirmation that you're not alone as stated before.

There's always someone out there in this vast world at some point in time that has needed this type of help, or is possibly in need of it right now. If my assistance can help just one person out there to make it through, then I've done what God has petitioned me to do. In doing so, this is my obedience to the Lord.

If there was always a sweet success story, there would be no need for the Bible, or a need for anyone to write books to try and help others. Take a look at **Genesis 22: 1-2:** "And it came to pass after these things, that God did tempt Abraham, and said unto him, Abraham: and he said, Behold, *here* I *am*." **Verse 2**: "And he said, Take now thy son, thine only *son* Isaac, whom thou lovest, and get thee into the land of Moriah; and offer him there for a burnt offering upon one of the mountains which I will tell thee of."

What a great sacrifice! Now, God did not ask that you sacrifice a child or anything of that nature. He only asked you to sacrifice a portion of your finances in a timely manner (being obedient). However, that never happened. You didn't obey God. Then a chain of events began to lead you into a difficult way. What was not a problem at the beginning when there was excess, became a problem, now becoming a great sacrifice. Your excess changed to a need, thus making you feel you want to hold on tight to what you have.

You must remember there was sacrifice from the beginning of time. There was sacrifice when God sacrificed His son to bear the cross for all, in our sinful state. He bore all the pain of sin for the entire world so that we would have the right to the tree of life. Wow! What a blessing on high! Our sacrifice has nothing to do with death, or the giving up of a loved one. Besides, none of these things belong to us anyway. It all belongs to God. The Lord doesn't want to take anything away from you. He just wants to multiply your seed, giving it back to you. It's always more than what you had from the very beginning anyway.

Christ loves us all so much that He gave the greatest sacrifice in history! Nothing has ever matched it since the beginning of time. We could never beat that! Christ only wants to test our love for Him. So show Him that you love Him, too.

Whatever the case may be, just do it! Don't look back! Most of all, you must have a cheerful heart along with a desire. This allows confidence in your excitement to see what He'll do for you in return. I guarantee you can't match or beat His love for you.

Chapter IV

The Testing Of Your Faith

One of the most exciting, very powerful messages stands on a promise in the word of God. That message represents the "Tenth" — the "Tithe" — the 'first-fruits' of all your increase which God blesses you with. **Proverbs 3: 9-10:** says, "Honour the Lord with thy substance, and with the first fruits of all thine increase:" **Verse 10:** "So shall thy barns be filled with plenty, and thy presses shall burst out with new wine."

This message is surely the promise of God's blessing to you. The word tithe is a verb showing action. It is the act of bringing, along with giving. This does not mean to bring it with you, continuing to hold onto it, yet contemplating while rationalizing whether or not to give it.

Deuteronomy 12: 6: "And thither ye shall bring your burnt offerings, and your sacrifices, and your tithes, and heave offerings of your hand, and your vows, and your freewill offerings, and the firstlings of your herds and of your flocks:" Tell me, how hard is it to give back to God a very small portion of what He has given you? It's only a tenth, just a dime off of every dollar; it's His anyway. Understand that God doesn't need it. He wants us to obey, being willing to give that commanded portion back to Him as an act of faith. Therefore, He can multiply the seed sown for His kingdom back to you. The more you give, the more God has to work with to increase what you get in return.

It's like the farmer. Those of you who keep gardens, or have had the opportunity to work on a farm, will know exactly what I'm talking about. The fewer amount of seeds you sow, the less reaping there will be. The more seeds, the more you reap from your harvest. Isn't that right? You give generously, then your returns are bountiful! There are only two choices. There are no gray areas, no in-betweens. You either do it, or you don't.

If you choose to be obedient you will always walk with continued abundance and prosperous living. If you choose not to obey, then you'll walk under the curse of disobedience. There are no if's—no and's—no but's. There is absolutely no other way to put it.

Malachi 3: 10: "Bring ye all the tithes into the storehouse, that there may be meat in mine house, and prove me now herewith, saith the Lord of hosts, if I will not open you the windows of heaven, and pour you out a blessing, that *there shall* not *be room* enough *to receive it*." Now that's the power of the tithe. Not only does God promise to multiply your seed, blessing you, but He says to try Him, seeing whether or not He'll open the windows of heaven pouring out a blessing for you. That word 'blessing' in the singular state is so large that the Lord says: "He'll open up the windows of heaven to pour you out a blessing that you have not room enough to receive."

Based on my own experience in paying my tithes, giving persistently and consistently in the last few years, I feel that I've had some occasions to experience that verse to a certain degree. I say, 'certain degree' because I feel that God should not be limited. In believing this, I know that He has so much more for me. However, since I've been consistent in my tithes and giving of my offerings, my barn, and my storehouse are constantly running over. I have to turn blessings away, giving to others for the reason that there just isn't any room to receive some things. Hallelujah! The Lord also promises to take care of you in all of your ways and in all of your affairs.

Malachi 3: 11-12: "And I will rebuke the devourer for your sakes, and he shall not destroy the fruits of your ground; neither shall your vine cast her fruit before the time in the field, saith the Lord of hosts." **Verse 12:** "And all nations shall call you blessed: for ye shall be a delightsome land, saith the Lord of hosts." Listen! God means just what He says in His word. Whoever or whatever is trying to devour you, or anything that belongs to you will be stopped! Nothing and no one can destroy or take away any gift that God has given you. Now that doesn't mean that the enemy won't try, but he can't succeed. The devil always has plans, but that's all they are, just plans.

Let me share this testimony with you. God recently blessed me with a desire of my heart that I'd been praying about for approximately a year. It was my very own truck to be used for my ministry to carry items such as food, blankets, bibles, etc., for the homeless. It was top of the line, equipped with everything anyone's heart could desire. When the Lord blessed me with the increase, I went to get the truck, but I asked my sales agent to excuse me for a few minutes, because I had to write another check first. The first check had to be for the Lord, giving Him the first-fruit of my increase.

As I wrote that check I said, "Lord, I acknowledge that this increase is all because of you. I'm so very thankful for all you've done for me. To show you my appreciation, here are the first fruits, my gift seed offering. For you are Lord and I love you. My desire is to obey your will, your commandments. This seed I sow back into your kingdom says thank you from the very depths of my heart for blessing me." Before I wrote a check for anything, I had to give God back His portion first. Once I took possession I anointed that entire truck, praying for God's blessing over it. I also prayed for God's protection for myself, and also for those who might accompany me.

Approximately two months after having the new vehicle, it was parked in the parking lot at my job. Someone broke out the entire passenger window, got in, and tried to take the mounted television unit out of the ceiling. The taking of my property was not a success. It was a failed plan, having to be aborted.

My supervisors alerted me suggesting that I go see what happened. I wanted to cry so badly. My heart just sank. Remember, I said I wanted to cry, but the tears wouldn't come. I felt so bad because I'd invested a seed faith/gift offering to help a church which the Lord laid on my heart to do work for. Items for that project were in my vehicle as well.

There were hundreds of dollars worth of new items that I'd purchased and in addition to those purchases, there were other items for another job that I was working on for a very dear friend. I had quite a collection of new music, a VCR with headsets, and a very nice briefcase that contained many important papers.

Another thing that stands out in my mind was that I had my Bible on the seat on the side the person or persons entered. Now they would've had to cross over it to get to the other side. I want to believe that God spoke to their heart, or hearts. Hopefully that is what frightened them away, the reason they had to abort their little mission. I hope they were scared out of their wits and that they'll never forget that day. Somehow, I feel that little episode was a testimony and turning point in their lives.

While walking to my vehicle, I kept repeating to myself. "Now Lord, I know you wouldn't allow them to take any of the church's items, would you?" Well, the thought of that just made my heart sink deeper, but I really couldn't believe that He would allow that. Perhaps this is why the tears wouldn't come. It would have made my heart sick to know that those items could have been taken.

Once there, much to my surprise, the pliers that were used were still on the seat along with a small amount of bloodstained fingerprints. However, they could not remove the television unit or the mount. Best of all, they didn't take one item out of my truck. Hallelujah, Praise God! With each new day I can see the blessing of God in the ordeal. Tell me, who would not have taken a couple of big bags of new items, if they were out to do wrong?

I will always believe standing on the promise that God said He will rebuke the devourer for my sake and that He shall not destroy the fruits of my ground. It was a financial blessing and I am guilt-free in the Lord because of my obedience in giving the tenth of my first fruits from that blessing with which God blessed me. Now if we are going to prove God, we have to give Him something to work with, since it is our very own blessing that we are seeking.

Let's take another look at the farmer or gardener. Have you ever seen someone who has any amount of good sense plant something, then just sit there waiting for something to happen? No, of course not! If a farmer did that, he probably wouldn't produce very much. Even when he plants a lot of seeds, he still worries because there are no guarantees that his crop will yield a good harvest.

There are a lot of factors on which farmers and gardeners have to depend. It could be the weather, soil, temperatures, the amount of watering, etc. As a rule of thumb, all of those elements play a factor. However, with God, there is nothing but great dividends and returns all the time, regardless of the weather, temperature, or other natural elements or disasters. It doesn't matter if the weather turns bad or if we have a severe storm or frost or not enough rain. I'm here to tell you that these things do not stop God!

It doesn't matter if we've had a scorching heat wave or a flood. It doesn't matter if we've had an invasion of pests in our fields that destroyed all the fruits of our ground. It just does not matter with God and He will not be defeated! Please listen to me. I'm here to say once again that none of these things are obstacles for God. This doesn't matter to God. He can work in the midst of any problems. With Him, there is no worry. I mean nothing or no one can take away or destroy anything that God has planned for us, and wants to give us.

When you cheerfully return a portion of what you have to God, you can forget about it and walk away, then just watch God work on your behalf. Isn't it wonderful to have someone work on your behalf with your money, whom you can trust? First of all, He's honest. He won't take a penny of it because, as I said before, it all belongs to Him. He takes it, multiplies it, then returns it back to you at thirty, sixty or sometimes a hundred fold, depending on how much of it you entrusted to Him. How can you beat that? Even the bank's dividends aren't that great. Every time you get your hands on something, you need to be excited to give the Lord a portion, or tenth, of all your first-fruits and let God work with it on your behalf for your needs and desires.

There's something that bears repeating. I explained above the meaning of tithe. Tithe is a tenth of all your increase. There is a command and it is to give back to God right off the top. **Deuteronomy 8: 1:** "All the commandments which I command thee this day shall ye observe to do … ," this is part of your blessing to obey all aspects of the Bible, not just the ones that are conveniently picked out to meet your needs.

We have to meet God's need and that need is to have a burning desire for the work of His kingdom. By the way, if you don't want to be a part of it, you will not stop His work at all. There is always a willing vessel somewhere who wants to obey God and His word. He'll always find someone who has made a covenant or a commitment with Him to obey His word, and do His will. They will proceed to go on to receive the rewards, the dividends, and the blessings with all the promises of God.

Now, as I share with you all of the truths that are

so rich and deeply saturated in my spirit, it makes me feel that there is something very special about this friendship that draws a closeness that God can bring between us to share in this way. You'll desire to meet me to see who I am. Of course I'll always desire to meet all of my readers, knowing that you can't always go it alone. You'll be able to read about someone else's trials, their tribulations to gain their personal knowledge with their experiences, as not to make the same mistakes. This is always such a blessing to me.

Throughout this book I try to reassure, help, and comfort you in order to help you make the right choices and decisions. Please do not separate yourselves because isolation is a very bad thing. It can be the beginning of deterioration. As I said before, our faith is what brings us as close as we can be within these pages. It doesn't matter who or what you are or where you're from. God works through all types of people and right now we are all imperfect people.

It is faith that allows you to experience the impossible. It is the best way to live with your weaknesses and shortcomings. It is intended to shift your faith unto the power of God. Again, once you've made the decision to get out of the boat and start walking on the water, do not take your eyes off of God to look down at the water. What this means is: Do not look at your circumstances or your surroundings. Just remember that you are only a prayer away from the one who can actually help you. Hold onto God's unchanging hand. When there is no one else to turn to, the Lord will not fail to give you the support, the help, and the wisdom that you need to know the truth.

Whether you pick up the Bible to read it for yourself, or the Lord sends something or someone like me or this book for your confirmation, just be happy about it. Ultimately, it doesn't matter who tells you, it's what they tell you and how you receive it. You must look to God when the enemy comes against you.

Again, when all else fails, go back and read **Deuteronomy 7: 11-12:** "Thou shall therefore keep the commandments, and the statutes, and the judgments, which I command thee this day, to do them." **Verse 12:** "Wherefore it shall come to pass, if ye hearken to these judgments, and keep, and do them, that the Lord thy God shall keep unto thee the covenant and the mercy which he sware unto thy fathers:"

The Lord wants to establish a covenant with His believers for you and your affairs. We need to get this divine revelation of faith, prosperity, and abundant living, deeply saturated in our spirits. However, something is wrong when the bills are not getting paid and you can't meet your needs. The car is falling apart; you're barely making it to work to earn another paycheck. The refrigerator and the cupboards are bare. The children's clothes, as well as yours, are tired and worn.

Deprivation seems to be lurking within the boundaries of every wall. Ask yourself, "Is there a possibility that I'm not keeping all of the commandments?" If you have nagging debts, you need a better paying job, and if you seem to have obstacle after obstacle facing you every hour of every day, just ask this question, "Is there anything I can do to change my circumstances?"

Another question should be, "Am I continuing

to give my tithes along with offerings on a persistent and continuous basis?" If you're not, this next verse could very well be one possible reason.

Deuteronomy 8: 9: "A land wherein thou shalt eat bread without scarceness, thou shalt not lack any *thing* in it; a land whose stones *are* iron, and out of whose hills thou mayest dig brass." So if the answer to the question is, "No, I am not living this verse," then this is definitely the wrong answer! It's a major problem and, like I said, very possibly the reason for your lack. If you're not reaping the benefits and your response is not yes, then you are not letting God do what He desires and promised to do in your life.

Although if your answer is yes, then you should be living that verse and taking a positive step in faith and obeying the commandments of God. In doing so, it gives Him the go-ahead to look into your circumstances to get the spirit of lack off your back. If not, you have to contend with some very serious problems. **Malachi 3: 8-10:** "Will a man rob God? Yet ye have robbed me. But ye say, Wherein have we robbed thee? In tithes and offerings." **Verse 9:** "Ye *are* cursed with a curse: for ye have robbed me, *even* this whole nation." So, if you've been robbing God, then you will be cursed for not following and obeying God's word. His commandments are as simple as that.

Verse 10: "Bring ye all the tithes into the storehouse, that there may be meat in mine house, and prove me now herewith, saith the Lord of hosts, if I will not open you the windows of heaven, and pour you out a blessing, that *there shall* not *be room* enough *to receive it*." What an awesome promise! At this point, I encourage you to rush back and get into God's presence and His word to make things right. Don't hinder the fullness of God's blessings and benefits that He wants to manifest upon you and your family.

Throughout the book, I'll be sharing with you some things that happened to me regarding my disobedience, which prompted curses. Whether through fear, neglect, wavering in my faith, or whatever the reasons were, God frowns on our being disobedient. I will also share my acts of obedience due to the increase in my faith, along with benefits and all of the rewards. I will continue to share with you my progress and the things I encountered along the way as well as the obstacles and successes.

You know the Lord will prepare the way and see you through if you're obedient. He will not leave you or forsake you. We just need to be quiet at times and listen to His voice. I know there are times our tests seem so difficult and overwhelming that we become afraid. We begin to fall back into our old habits in order to feel secure, thus, continuing to have the need to feel, touch, or see things physically, with God being one of them.

Now at a time in our lives when we need to stand, especially at our weakest moments, what should we do? The title of my first book asks if we are "Trusting in God? Or trusting in self, others, or finances?" Ultimately, we begin to trust in the latter three, because we can see and physically touch them. We begin to feel secure in different types of things, except for the right things, such as the word of God and His promises. He promises to see us through. We need to believe that and hold onto it. Do you realize how it breaks the Lord's heart for us to turn our backs on Him and turn to another source that isn't even guaranteed?

Why are we so quick to trust in the word of man rather than God? When man promises to help us, to bail us out or loan us money, and makes all other sorts of promises, we just run with it and cling to every word and sometimes we even brag about it to others. The minute that goes haywire our whole world is shattered and we are set back even further than where we began. Most of the time, their words are only promises that are broken. Why? Because man is fallible, but when man does come through that often creates a debt that you must pay back. The big question sometimes is: "What do I get in return?"or "You'll owe me this or you'll need to do that."

Many times, most of the people in whom you place your trust will put your business in the street or they'll always remind you in some way all that they've done for you. With almost a certainty, there will be some who will purposely share with someone else in some small bragging way what it is they have done for you. You do know what I'm talking about, don't you? Can you be a witness to that? I can tell you this without a shadow of a doubt: God is not like that. He never breaks His promises. Whatever He promises, He does. He never keeps a running tally or an IOU sheet up in heaven for all the angels to see, nor does He gossip. May I ask, have you ever known God to lie? Well, He will not lie because He cannot lie. If He hasn't answered yet, it's only because it's not His season or timing.

One very real factor is that you can't always trust in or depend on man. Things can often happen out of our control. However, it is in God's control to do any and everything for anyone at all times, keeping His word, always. Why wouldn't He, especially when we're doing what He wants us to do? As in His promise, His word will not return void. Just remember, the devil is a liar, a con artist, and a deceiver; consequently it takes daily prayer to turn your life completely over to God.

The minute you think you've finally got it right, something happens in your life to throw you for a loop. It doesn't matter how small the battle might be; always turn everything over to God. Trust in Him, not in your resources. That should always be your motto. Remember, your stuff can be here today and gone tomorrow. We know this, so why do we forget? We have to know that anything and everything can happen to wipe it all out completely. I bring these things up time and time again throughout this book because these are things we need to remember. In reality, your life carries a chain of events that are tests and great feats for you to accomplish. Hopefully, you'll pass each test in order to be raised to each new level.

Let me share another testimony with you. During church one Sunday, a visiting minister challenged all of us to obey God in the very special way that He was moving in each of our hearts. It was a test that was to prove to be only the beginning of a series of tests with which I was going to have to do battle. Why couldn't I just be obedient and make life easier? Well, the chain of events started very rapidly and I seemed to be in a whirlwind of decisions as I tried to pass the test of obedience. These things are usually very familiar, because they're things that you've read about, but didn't have an understanding of, although you knew you needed to be delivered. Then God sends someone along with more experience in the word, and it just happens to be what you need to know at that particular moment and place in order to prepare for your future.

I really thought at this point in my life things were a little more secure and wrapped up than they were. I was basically a new member of my church, just beginning to settle in and feeling very excited about the Lord, His word, and very anxious to be obedient, or so I thought. I was very tired of my life being in a mediocre state. Whatever His word told me to do, I knew that if properly done with all diligence and obedience, it would work. However, I soon learned that although the spirit was willing, the flesh was very, very weak. During the course of the offering on that particular day, the minister asked for us to step out on faith and stretch, stretch, stretch to give. We were asked to give an amount over and above what we would normally give.

I didn't have much money this particular Sunday. Therefore, I took the very last dollar that I thought I had and placed it in a tithe and offering envelope. At that point, I was very hurt, wishing deep in my heart that I had more to give and actually, I did. Besides the one dollar, I also had forty dollars in my purse. It was to be used to pay a bill that was past due. I was going to pay it on Monday as part of a payment arrangement. I can honestly tell you that I pondered and pondered over the forty dollars, wondering if God would really see me through my ordeal. While sitting there, I began to pray and ask God what I should do.

Through that prayer, I believed God was speaking to me, giving me His hand saying, ***"Step out of***

the boat and trust Me to meet all of your needs." Glory to God! The Lord wanted at that moment to change the course of events in my life that always made the same old history for me. The spirit of the Lord began to move within me and I felt that this really was God definitely speaking to my heart, so I had to do it. Yes, I was afraid to do it because that bill had to be paid, and if memory serves me right, there was already an extension on that bill, so I really needed to get it paid right away. However, I was more afraid of not obeying God than I was of not paying that bill. I needed to start something new with God that I had never done before and that was to trust Him for everything and not in my finances, in others, or in myself.

One thing that should be very clear and important in our lives is that we need to completely obey God and His word about tithing and offerings. Therefore, I decided to give the forty dollars instead of the one dollar so I ripped open that envelope quickly and removed the dollar bill and replaced it with the forty dollars. This sacrifice was such a giant step that it was going to ultimately change the course of my life's events, finally making things different for me. Events continued to happen in my life, but whenever God blessed me, I gave Him His portion right off the top.

Now, at the first sign of getting back on course when you know that God is moving, thus blessing you, don't just sit back in your easy chair, getting comfortable, ceasing to pray. Continue to hold on until your change has been completed. When you start to hold onto God's unchanging hand, the devil will get mad, starting to work overtime, making up his little schemes along the way. The Lord is counting on you, but so is the devil; he's counting on you to fail. The devil wants to make God along with you both liars, but tell him, *it's not so!*

Now after passing the first test on that Sunday, not more than a day or so passed when I received an unexpected check in the mail. It was for more than a thousand dollars. Blessed be the name of the Lord! He gave me back what I'd given out, plus a lot more than I could ever have dreamed. He went before me, regarding that situation, working it out for me. I was so excited, astounded, and I might add, very happy and grateful. I was in a state of awe at what God had done for me. It was the most unexpected surprise.

When God produces for you, don't just take it in stride as though He owes you something. Let the miracles that God does for you harvest a personal relationship between you and Him, sharing your testimony with the world. You see, we all need confirmations from time to time. He wants to bond with you, so let Him! He only does things for you because He loves you!

Have you ever thought about the fact that the Lord has no boundaries as to what He'll do for you? You will come to realize that His blessings are endless as long as you're obedient. So, therefore I'm sharing with you just a few of His endless boundaries. Now, just because I received that check didn't mean I was on easy street.

Soon after, a series of other tests for other levels of achievement in the Lord just happened to come my way. These are just avenues that lead to greater things for you if you are obedient. It can come one step at a time, unless you are an overachiever in obedience, then blessings come to you by leaps and bounds. The key word here is obedience. You can live in abundance, fruitfully and victoriously in prosperous living.

Prior to this test, I desired something special and, of course, it was very expensive and I really couldn't afford it. It was a car. I had never really owned one and I wanted to have my very own; this being a few years before the purchase of my truck. At that time I was driving a leased vehicle, only one year down with four years to go, upside down I might say. Yet, I was going to continue trusting in God and step out on faith no matter what anyone said, dealerships, salesmen, and so forth. The dealerships really wanted me to lease the new car that I wanted, but that would have made the car payment almost as much as my mortgage, plus, I'd be in the hole owing a lot of money on the return of the other leased car.

Months went by, knowing in my heart it would definitely take a miracle from God, but if anyone could put me in the car that I wanted, He surely could and would. This particular day the car had not been on my mind. However, the Lord redirected my steps in the process of going home. The Spirit of the Lord ushered my spirit to continue to drive straight and as I drove, I prayed and asked the Lord what this was all about. I finally came to a section of town where there was nothing but rows upon rows, block after block of car dealerships. I knew now in my spirit that I was to look for the car. I knew the color that I wanted, so I just began to look for only that color.

I had also prayed and given God precise information about the car that I desired to own—the color, make, model, as well as the tires, rims, interior type, and it also needed to have tinted windows. Those were some of the specifics that I had in mind. My head was going left to right, back and forth, again and again, covering both sides of the street. I asked the Lord to direct me. Finally, I saw the nose of a car that was the exact color that I was looking for, but I couldn't quite make out the type, as I had gotten only a glimpse of it. I made a quick U-turn at the intersection, pulled in and parked. Right there, in the middle of a truck lot, was my dream car. As I found out later, the prior owners were an elderly couple; the reason for the low mileage.

God, being the architect He is, designed this car exactly to all of my specifications, even more so than I had ever imagined. Isn't God something? Would you have ever done it that way? No, probably not. It was tucked away on a truck lot just for me. Through my obedience, I found the gift. If I hadn't obeyed, it would have been given to someone else moving at the right time, God's time. I'm sure I wasn't the only one interested in a car like that; however, I wouldn't have gone to a truck lot to look for it either.

Embracing God and what He had done for me, I began to see a vision of a very large gift, wrapped so nice with a big pretty red bow on top, and God handing it to me saying, "This is for you, my child, because I love you." I began to run around this car, over and over again, crying and praising God for I knew with all my heart that this car was for me.

Finally, I ran to the window to see if I could find a price. I couldn't believe my eyes. There were two signs on the car, a regular sale sign and a "blow out" sale sign. In other words, the car was marked down twice. A young man finally came out, I'm sure to see what the excitement and commotion was all about. When he finally got me to calm down, he asked me if everything was all right. I replied, "Yes!" and in the very same breath I stated to him, "This is my car!" Of course, he looked at me with amazement and said, "Okay?" He asked if I wanted to talk about it and I answered, "Yes."

We went inside, talked a little, and he asked me if I had any money to put down on the car. I quickly gave that some thought, thinking the down payment had never crossed my mind, so I advised him, "Not yet." He asked me, "Then how can you expect me to hold the car?" At that moment, the Lord whispered to my spirit. "There's money in your purse." I had forgotten all about that money because it had been there for quite some time. One hundred dollars was tucked away in the bottom. Praise God!

You know the salesman was just as shocked as I was, especially since I had just told him that I didn't have it yet. Perhaps he thought I was a magician or something. Oh, I'm something alright, once again I am a "*child of the King*." Then he took me for a long test drive, and wow, it was absolutely great! This was definitely the car for me. We went back to his office and talked some more. I asked if a hundred dollars could hold the car and he said, "Yes." So I gave him the money.

I went home rejoicing, but continued praying and asking the Lord how He was going to direct me because I was literally broke. Throughout my prayer, the Lord didn't say or give me much of anything to go on. A few months prior to this miracle, an unusual turn of events had occurred in my life. An unexpected event took place that meant a blessing for me, but I didn't want to depend on it, because I wasn't sure that it would happen at that particular time.

Within a matter of days, that particular blessing came to pass for me, right on time. The blessing depended greatly on an act of obedience about five years prior to this event. It was a very, very big blessing, yet an unexpected one. Once I received it, the Lord advised me as to what to do and how to do it. Sometimes the Lord has other things in mind as well. For example, He may want you to use the blessings for other gifts and blessings if it's your time and season.

I went back to the dealership with the specific instructions and the amounts with which to do business. The floor manager came in to work this particular deal because he wasn't very pleased with what I had to offer. I think he felt that because I was a female I probably didn't know much about the business and thought he could possibly take advantage of me. This could very well have been the case, but since I had instructions from God there was no way to persuade me otherwise.

After a while, it got a little more personal. It began to be a battle between the devil and myself. We sat at opposite ends of the table and he stared me in the face, eye-to-eye. I looked right through him, discerning his spirit. It was the enemy himself. It was as though he had a mask on his face and in looking beyond the mask I could see something that was not the person sitting before me. It was battling with my spirit in silence and no one knew what was going on. It was toying with my mind, speaking very harsh words in silence. It said, "You will never get this car, and he would make sure of that. Nothing you can say or do will change that." In my thoughts, I rebuked the devourer and was pleading the blood of Jesus. I was in total shock as to what was happening before my eyes.

Why wouldn't the dealership want to sell me the car? Of course, you know it wasn't about that at all. It was about the blessing that was bestowed upon me. The devil wanted me to blow it, or to give up, to cause me to look at the situation and not remember God's promises and what He said He would do for me. Before I left, I looked that man in the face and promised him that I was not going to give up. I was going to get that car and I would be back.

I drove home, crying all the way, asking God what that was all about and what did He want me to do next? Well, the Father didn't answer right away. Besides, did you know that you can always hear God better in silence? Although God did come to me later in the night, during my sleep, and gave me more specific instructions. So you see what had occurred earlier was yet another test of my faith and my obedience. Even though the gift was already given, the blessing was not yet sealed.

The Lord advised me to go to a particular credit union, the exact location, what to pay down, how much the payments were to be, and how long to extend the payments. He also advised me about how much to put in the bank to open my own personal accounts, both checking and savings. I wondered how I was going to do this when I didn't have an existing account there and had never done business there in the past. The Lord didn't answer my next set of questions either. He just left it at that.

I went to the credit union and a lady assisted

me. She asked me if I had an account there and I told her, "No." She said, "Wait, there's an account here under your name." She asked me about the other name on the account, which was my son's. I had forgotten all about the account that I had co-signed on for him some years prior. It was now paid in full and left in good standing. Everything was a go; the credit union financed the car and everything worked out perfectly. I got a check for the amount I needed for the car. I called my salesman and advised him to get my new car ready because I would be there in a few hours to pick it up. I'm telling you, I couldn't wait to see their faces.

The next set of instructions the Lord gave me was to see the general manager at the dealership where I was leasing the car that I was currently driving. I did that right away. When I saw him, he said he remembered me and asked me what he could do for me. I told him I wanted him to take the lease back and why, giving all the explicit details that God had given me; to tell the truth. Now, you know that everyone I shared this with thought I was absolutely out of my mind. Surely the dealership would **not** take back a four-year lease with only one year down unless it was a situation of repossession. He looked at me and said, whatever he could do to make me happy, he'd do it. Now this is what I mean about catching God's wave, moving when he says to move in His timing.

Is God good or what? I get happy just thinking about it. However, he asked me if he could at least try to sell me another car to keep me as their customer. Of course, I was not going to be rude. I looked at the car he had in mind, test driving it to be polite. I apologized, turning down his offer, but asked him not to be offended because my heart was really set on the other car. He said he understood. We finished up all of the paperwork and he offered to have one of his best guys drive me to pick up my new car. How about that? I am telling you that I got the *red carpet treatment*. The young man asked the manager what car he should use to drive me to the other dealership. The manager told him to use the same car that we had test driven because it was nice and clean. He walked me out and wished me well with my new endeavors, and I thanked him.

During the ride to the other dealership, the young man driving asked me, rather emphatically, "Who are you?" I gave him my name and he asked me again, "I mean who are you really?" I asked him what would make him ask me such a question. He stated that he'd never seen any manager roll out the red carpet for anyone like that before in that type of situation. He said I must have held a very high rank or a prestigious title or something. I told him I did—*I am a child of the King*. Then I began to witness to him. I tell you, I gave that young man something to really think about for the rest of the day. That young man was in awe as he left with his mouth gaping in disbelief.

When I arrived to pick up my new car, they were all waiting but the look on the manager's face was one of defeat. He didn't come to congratulate me or say anything to me whatsoever. He watched me every step of the way, from the time I got there until the time I drove off the lot in my new car. By the end of the day, it felt so good and uplifting just to have passed all of my tests. It was a great feeling to have been obedient, receiving all the benefits and rewards, but then there are those greater rewards. The harder the tests, the greater the rewards, but this is all very good. It's for our making, and it strengthens our faith and takes us to the next level.

Chapter V

God's Instruction And Your Obedience

Obedience means to obey. It is the act or practice of obeying laws, rules, or requests. It is also the initial act of doing what has been taught or suggested, when accepted by someone in authority. Sometimes it results from some sort of persuasion. The quality or condition of being obedient could mean to carry out a request, command, or demand while being submissive, compliant and docile, yet still amiable. This form of obedience indicates accountability with responsibility. Being tractable means having the capacity of being handled or led. Being dutiful signifies an interest with reliability in carrying out what is specifically assigned or required. So with all of the explanations about being obedient, we are given opportunity for choice. **Deuteronomy 8: 1,20:** "All the commandments which I command thee this day shall ye observe to do, that ye may live, and multiply, and go in and possess the land which the Lord sware unto your fathers." **Verse 20:** "As the nations which the Lord destroyeth before your face, so shall ye perish; because ye would not be obedient unto the voice of the Lord your God." There will ultimately be death and destruction to deaf ears. Will you decide today whom you will serve?

Joshua 24: 15: "And if it seem evil unto you to serve the Lord, choose you this day whom ye will serve; whether the gods which your fathers served that *were* on the other side of the flood, or the gods of the Amorites, in whose land ye dwell: but as for me and my house, we will serve the Lord." I beg of you to make the right decision today. There is no in between with God. It is either "Yes, Lord, I will!"—or—"No, Lord, I won't!" You're either going to obey, or not, or you're probably stuck somewhere right in the middle. However, God will not have you stuck in the middle of whether to obey Him or the other voice.

Revelations 3: 15-16: "I know thy works, that thou art neither cold nor hot: I would thou wert cold or hot." **Verse 16:** "So then because thou art lukewarm, and neither cold nor hot, I will spue thee out of my mouth."

Let's explore this a little more in depth. There may be a few of you whom I could possibly help now, or perhaps in the future. First, there were the tests, then there were certain prayers that were prayed asking God for specific gifts and callings. Now perhaps God might have been ready for you to rise up to another level in Him and maybe you set out to do what you were instructed by God to do, and didn't quite make it after asking God to bless you with that something in particular. Often times, many of us pray to receive something from God, but when He gives it to us, sometimes we run from it, leaving it behind.

Can you believe the nerve of some of us? So, ultimately, when we do this, what are we saying? "Oh, Lord, am I really ready at this time? Give me a little more time. Lord, you moved too fast. Can you give me time to think about this? I'm scared that I might make a big mistake. What will people say or think?"

Whatever the case may be, or your thoughts have been, or might be at this very crucial moment, if you're being honest, you'll admit having dealt with at least one of those scenarios once in your lifetime. This is why you need to be very careful what you ask God to give you or do for you. You need to know if this is what you really want. You need to be ready to accept it when God comes calling on you, requesting you to go forth or to do something.

Now, let's go back to being careful about what you ask for from God. You need to be quite sure, and ready when you first go to Him, ready to accept the plan that He has for you. When He's moving and the anointing is flowing, you are given a chance to flow with it, acting in faith upon what God is telling you to do. So when you don't obey the first time, He may not give it to you in the same manner the second time. If so, there would be no need for faith. However, with His loving kindness and forgiving ways, He shows us His mercy, abounding His grace upon us with His promises. **Romans 11: 29:** "For the gifts and calling of God *are* without repentance."

If some of you have gone through this type of experience and didn't quite make it, get up, dust yourself off, asking God for His divine forgiveness so He can forgive you. You know He will. God will give you another chance, but in His own season and timing. You see with God, it's about faith, and it's about love, too. Do you really love Him?

Most likely, every experience will not be the same. You might have to go through more tests and trials, unlike the ones you've gone through before for the same gift in this area. Since that time of my inability to be obedient, there had been quite a struggle, but I refused to give up. I felt that if I didn't continue, I'd really upset God and I didn't want to do that. I believed when the time came, God would manifest Himself again.

The Lord is mighty, magnificent, and awesome. He demands respect. There comes a time when He will not settle for anything else, only getting down to business.

Because of this, my faith was beginning to assume its position in Christ Jesus. One day, after work, still thinking about the experience I had on that previous Sunday, as I went into my room to change my clothes, I had an overwhelming feeling that I perceived from the Lord ushering me into His presence. I knelt beside the bed and began to pray. Upon submitting myself to the Lord, I began to feel God's presence and this great warmth engulfed me.

As the Lord began to take me far away on a journey, the Spirit took full control as I began to yield. Lo and behold! The Lord took me out in the midst of a body of water in a boat, a very small boat, or perhaps it was so much water that the boat just seemed tiny.

The Lord began to ask me some very serious questions, such as: "Do you trust me? Do you love me? Then if you do, take my hand, step out of the boat unto the water, and trust me." Hallelujah, Glory to God, in the Highest! How could you resist something like that? Well, if you can't, then you can imagine what happened next. I did it! I was actually standing on the water!

After all that I had been through, I knew in my spirit to keep my eyes on the Lord and not to look down. As long as I didn't look at my current circumstances or situation, I knew I would be fine. The Lord was so proud of my achievements. Therefore, being obedient and totally trusting in God helped me to pass this test and it would surely help me to pass other tests. Read *TRUSTING GOD* ? for the tests that followed.

So please keep me in your prayers and I'll do the same for you. For we will be overcomers in the Lord together. I am here to help you through the rough times that you may be going through. It could possibly be the same thing that I've had to go through, or something similar. Perhaps you may know of someone who is going through these same experiences, so please share this wealth of information with them.

My words of encouragement to you would be: 'Welcome God to be your divine leader, orchestrating all of your affairs.' After all, He is an all-knowing, all-seeing God. He knows what is going to happen; what is down the road and around the corner. Therefore, He has your best interests in mind. Why not let God take hold of the reins and let Him be the driver.

Admit it! You know He's a better driver. Allow Him to do what's best for you. His will is always perfect, with no strings attached, no price to pay. Just remember that satan's little perks with benefits, that some call blessings, are all only temporary. They're cheap, coming a dime a dozen. They can cost you your very life.

They're fake—imitation, not real. They look pleasing to the eye, gazing through those rose colored glasses, but they're only water-colored lies. They will eventually fade away, with his promises falling through the cracks.

So when we do not obey God's commandments or listen to His instructions, it is a no-win situation. The devourer with all of his mess that he entangles you in, such as being disobedient, not listening to God, is going to make you pay for your choices. If you don't repent and get on the right track, you're making the devil your choice. Make God your choice today. Choose to listen, moving when He tells you to move.

Don't miss out, letting the devil steal all of your joy, taking your gifts because he's the father of all lies. He doesn't want them, but he doesn't want you to have them either. No matter how many times you hear this message, just remember God loves you so much and it is His will for all to be saved.

Choose Christ this day. I chose to put my life on hold to spread the gospel, which is the good news of Jesus Christ and when you tell of His goodness and what He's done for you, it's very rewarding and you never get tired of it. Try God, give Him a chance. Don't miss your divine appointment. He's doing it for others, and wants to do the same for you. He wants to be your divine leader, the head of your life preparing, leading, guiding you in all your ways.

The devil is a master deceiver. As I said before, he's sly, slick, witty, and cunning. He's out to rob, kill, and destroy. He doesn't care about you or anything that belongs to you. He doesn't care how he takes you out, he just has to do something, anything, no matter what, even if it means actually taking your life. His time is very limited, so he wants to take down as many as he possibly can. He doesn't want to reside in hell for all eternity by himself.

Satan has a point, and wants to prove it to God. What he doesn't want to believe is that **Jesus already has the victory, and He has already won the battle**. So the devil has his own high hopes with just plans. Guess what, that's all they are—hopes and plans. You must desire to be on the winning side to have eternal life, to reign with our Lord and Savior Jesus Christ.

I tell my children as much as I possibly can, don't just get right, stay right. I want all of us to be in heaven together. However, if any of my children choose not to make Jesus Christ their Lord and Savior, then I choose not to give Him up for the sake of loving them and vice versa. They don't have a heaven or hell to put me in, neither does anyone else on this earth. No one loves me like my Father in heaven, no one.

He is the source of my joy and my everything. I have no other desire than to please Him, although there have been times that I've stumbled and not passed my test. I pray never to give up on Christ, as He has never given up on me. Therefore, if I should stumble, I pray to continue to get up, brush myself off, and try over and over again until I can get it right.

God doesn't want to turn His back on us or turn a deaf ear either. He is always there for us, no matter where or when, and no matter what. Make your choice and choose who you will serve because you know not the time or the day of the return of the Lord. Will you be ready?

Do you love God? Well then, show Him. Make Him happy and proud as you would a father. God examines your heart and not your works. So keep a blessed heart, staying humble and loving Him as if it's the very first time you've accepted Him into your life. Don't let Him down. Don't let what the devil says about you be the truth, because he's a liar and the truth is not in him. Get happy, because we have choices.

We can walk around openly and worship and praise God when we want to, and the way we want to do it. Yes, you've fallen, and you'll probably fall again, but don't turn your back on God. He's the one who will see you through and make you free. He's the one who picks His children up.

Have you ever noticed satan picking you up after a fall? No, of course not!

He just stands there with his foot on your neck, trying to hold you down, until you give up and lose. What kind of God is this? See him for who he is, and that's nobody. Even your friends sometimes aren't there to pick you up, but the true and living God never fails. He'll never leave you or forsake you. He'll stand by you even if your best friend lets you down.

When your mother or father lets you down, even when your sisters, your brothers, and your own children let you down, He'll stand by you. What I'm trying to say is: man is fallible. There are times they just can't be where we need them to be, or when we need them to be there. Sometimes it's very hard for them to keep their promises.

They don't mean to be that way; that's just the way it is. My Lord and Savior Jesus Christ, the God in whom I trust, is a God who never sleeps. He's never too busy or tired for you to call on Him. His line is never busy.

He'll never give you voice prompts, then put you on hold to never return to the line again, with you hearing a busy signal. You'll never get voice mail and a message saying: after the sound of the beep, please leave your name, number, and a brief message, I'll get back to you at my earliest convenience.

He doesn't have to call up someone else, or three-way your call to get someone in the middle (a lead or a supervisor) to help, or get approval to do His job, causing your business to be put on the street or all over town. My God would never use call waiting right in the midst of your emergency and put you on hold to take another call. God doesn't have caller ID; He doesn't need it! When you call, He recognizes who you are, and remembers that you've called several times already.

He will never ignore the call with a recorded message saying your card has expired, or you've used up all your minutes, call this 1-800 number using your credit card to add additional minutes; thus, never taking your call. You'll never have to worry about calling Him from a pay phone, to be disconnected before you've explained the problem or getting cut off in the midst of a conversation, having to call back collect because you ran out of money or didn't have enough coins.

The God we serve is a good God. He's a right now God, a God who is always there! Praise God, Hallelujah! He always knows before there is. God works on your behalf. He's a 'take care of business' kind of God who doesn't file things away in the next day bin or put off til tomorrow what He can do today.

He's a **911** God, rightfully bearing his name! He's faithful, loyal, and legitimate, not counterfeit, fake or a cheap imitation. He would never place you on hold to hear another language that you couldn't understand because He knows you. Besides, He is the author of all languages.

You'll never have to listen to some bizarre music in a time of distress when your need is now! He'd never transfer you to three or four different departments, and by the time you get through to the right one there isn't a need anymore (too late).

You'll never find that because of His busy day, He's too tired and doesn't want to deal with your problems therefore, accidentally disconnecting, leaving you to hear the 'flatline.' Are you familiar with this? When there's an emergency with His children and their affairs, God gives prompt, major medical attention.

He doesn't turn you away because you may not have insurance or the funds to pay, neither because of race, creed, or color. None of these things matter to God. Glory Hallelujah, Praise His Holy Name!

How many of you usually eat at five-star restaurants or stay at five-star hotels? You could never make a bad choice if you do. There are so many choices to be made. Everything is excellent. Whatever choice you make, you can't go wrong, unlike the decision I'm asking you to make today. There are not a lot of choices to be made here. There are only two: "God"—(Heaven, and Eternal life) or "satan"—(hell, death, and destruction).

The choice used here in comparison with a five-star restaurant is God, but He's far greater, and nothing can compare. **Psalms 34: 8:** "O taste and see that the Lord *is* good..." He is far better than any delicacy. On the other hand tasting of the devil is disaster, and in no way a comparison to a non five-star hotel or restaurant. It's much, much worse; it is death and hell!

Whereby, if you've read anything about heaven, you know it exceeds any stretch of the imagination regarding the design and comfort of any hotel or restaurant. **Psalms 89: 6:** "For who in the heaven can be compared unto the Lord…?"

Or would you like hell to be your home? Now you make the choice. Choose life or death. If you choose life, there are great rewards, dividends, and other great returns. In making your decision, I'm sure it would be in your best interest, because you love the Lord and you believe that He is Lord.

However, you need to be in love with the Lord enough to also reach out and share the love of God to others.

All the Lord wants is for us to love Him. He loves us so much, and wants us to love and share His love with the entire world. Whatever capacity that has been given to you, use it to help others! There are so many out there who haven't had the chance to make their choice to choose Him. However, in **St. John 11: 35:** "Jesus wept." This is the shortest verse in the Bible, but it is powerful! Stay mindful that we can grieve the Holy Spirit and we don't want to do that. When we love, and truly love, the rest will follow. Remember that Christ loves you more than life itself. God's love is unconditional and God calls us all. Those who love Him are hereby called to preach, teach, or to deliver in any form the Gospel of the Good News. We are called to evangelize in some form or another.

Now there comes a time in your life where

there are no more excuses. I answered my calling, in making the decision to work for the Lord and win souls for Him. In addition, God has called me to write books for Him and get His message across, here and abroad.

Henceforth, I believe that in every bit of information that we're receiving from God himself there is definitely a need for His word in all forms.

This lets me know that God is using His people everywhere. Thus, the things I'm writing are very crucial, because it's being told in every form, and direction, using different sources. Just keep in mind that the Lord will enlarge your boundaries and increase your territories. He'll send you coast to coast. What a way to reach God's people. Praise God!

Chapter VI

Love For God

Love for God is your devotion and adoration for Him. This love depicts a special attachment that a servant may have toward his master, under whose dominance he wishes to remain. We love the master as a son loves his father. **Deuteronomy 6: 5:** "And thou shalt love the Lord thy God with all thine heart, and with all thy soul, and with all thy might."

Deuteronomy 10: 12: "And now, Israel, what doth the Lord thy God require of thee, but to fear the Lord thy God, to walk in all his ways, and to love him, and to serve the Lord thy God with all thy heart and with all thy soul," **II Thessalonians 3: 5:** "And the Lord direct your hearts into the love of God, and into the patient waiting for Christ." To love expresses the essential nature of God. To see God's love being demonstrated was found in the gift of His son who went to the cross to die for all of our sins. Can you see the magnitude of God's love in His actions?

That's what makes this love so different and so special. It's an exercise of the divine will and a deliberate choice made without cause, such as: "I'll love you, if you love me." This was not the case of God, because He first loved us. Therefore, Christian love has God for its primary object, and expresses itself first of all in obedience to His will, and to His word. The next step is to awaken your hearts. I just couldn't go on without talking about the greatest gift of all.

To love God also means to have a personal committed relationship with Him. God wants His time. He needs to be the head of your life, the one you awaken to, because it's surely not your clock, your husband, or your wife. Without Him, we are nothing, and we need to live our lives remembering that fact. We need Him in the morning, the noonday, even in the night after the sun goes down.

We are so quick to call on the name of the Lord or the name of Jesus whenever something goes wrong, and He is always there. How about being there for the Lord, sometimes just doing what He's calling you to do? It's not very hard to love Him. Every day we find and meet someone who comes into our lives that we think we like. How long does it take before we are head over heels for that person, and we really know nothing about them?

Then we allow that person full access to our lives and everything we are all about. We breathe them. We daydream constantly about them. They're with us in our sleep, in our dreams. In thinking about them constantly, we're always picking up the phone to call them in the wee hours of the night, early in the morning, even throughout the day. Well, this is the type of love we need to have for God.

We need to write Him love letters, tell Him, how much we love Him, how awesome He is and let Him know how much we appreciate all He's done for us. We need to dream about Him and the work of His kingdom and what we can do to please and assist Him. We need to think about the Lord and pray continuously to Him regarding all things.

What I'd really like to accomplish is helping you gain more knowledge and understanding on how to channel your energies to do less and allow God to do so much more. **Proverbs 3: 6:** "In all thy ways acknowledge him, and he shall direct thy paths." He didn't say "in some, or part"... but rather God is saying, "In all thy ways." Those words mean in everything we set out to do, He will give us direction. This means to direct, tell, or show you what or how to do something, whenever or whatever it is.

He's just waiting for you to ask Him for His help. Even something as ordinary as what to wear or even what to eat. How many of you pray and ask the Lord for direction with those kinds of things? Try it sometimes. You'd be amazed and pleasantly surprised at how God loves to be needed. He can't wait to keep His promise, helping to direct your paths.

What is needed to be said again is that the Lord has all the time in the world for His children. Not just a handful of us, but all of us individually. I can't say it enough, that Christ loves each and every one of you so much. When God gave up His son to die on the cross, don't you think that was very painful? He had to turn His back, with all of the crying out, the pain, and the suffering, because of the love He had for His son and us.

We need to give God the honor and glory, offering up what is rightfully His; You and I. We belong to Him. **Psalms 24: 1:** "The earth *is* the Lord's and the fulness thereof; the world, and they that dwell therein." We are reminded in having our close, intimate relationship with God. We need to miss God and the fellowship we have with Him, in the same manner we do with our loved ones.

You need to be alone with Him in your quiet time, in your secret closet. Just you and God, so you can hear Him. You can talk to Him and let Him know just how much you really love Him. **I Corinthians 13: 13:** "And now abideth faith, hope, charity, these three; but the greatest of these *is* charity." Just remember, God is Love.

Chapter VII

Fear Of God

Fear of God is an extreme reverence, to respect and love God, awe. Awe is a feeling of fear, wonder or respect, inspired by something or someone mighty and majestic, as toward a supreme power. It is a state of, or condition of, alarm or dread, used to describe the reaction, evoked in men by God's power; His mighty works of destruction and sovereignty, a divine act.

A reverential fear of God, unlike the intimidation caused by your adversaries, is a positive controlling factor or motive of one's life, in matters both spiritual and moral. It's not only the mere fear of His power, righteousness and retribution; it's much more than that. It's a 'wholesome dread' of displeasing the Lord!

Psalms 115: 13: "He will bless them that fear the Lord, *both* small and great." **Joshua 24: 14:** "Now therefore fear the Lord, and serve him in sincerity and in truth: and put away the gods which your fathers served on the other side of the flood, and in Egypt; and serve ye the Lord." Let's take another look at the scriptures to get a divine understanding. **Isaiah 8: 13:** "Sanctify the Lord of hosts himself, and *let* him *be* your fear, and *let* him be *your* dread."

Ecclesiastes 12: 13: "Let us hear the conclusion of the whole matter: Fear God, and keep his commandments: for this *is* the whole *duty* of man." **Deuteronomy 13: 4:** "Ye shall walk after the Lord your God, and fear him, and keep his commandments, and obey his voice, and ye shall serve him, and cleave unto him." The list goes on and can be addressed to a much greater degree or extent for study.

In life, we need something or someone in authority to regulate and control, to exercise in our lives, rules and regulations for us to abide by. We need all these things, because there are times we do not wish to conform, to do what is right! In the carnal, if we're given an inch, we *will* take a mile.

Adam and Eve proved that very point in the beginning of time. They were given everything imaginable. They were allowed to come and go as they pleased. Their life as we know it was of perfection, lacking nothing essential to the whole. It was without fault, flaws, or defects, excellent, and delightful in all aspects, being pure and undaunted. Perfect in all its completion, it satisfied all requirements, except for **curiosity**.

They could have anything and eat everything, with the exception of one thing that God had forbidden! **Genesis 2: 15-17:** "And the Lord God took the man, and put him into the garden of Eden to dress it and to keep it." **Verse 16:** "And the Lord God commanded the man, saying, Of every tree of the garden thou mayest freely eat:"

Verse 17: "But of the tree of the knowledge of good and evil, thou shalt not eat of it: for in the day that thou eatest thereof thou shalt surely die."

With everything being perfect, the feeling of

curiosity continued to overtake their sense of judgment. When this happens, greed often sets in. Now, their act of being curious was not a flaw, defect, or imperfection. God gave them the freedom of choice, based on love and trust, having to combine that with initiating and setting forth an order or command, but He didn't stop there; He forbade them, giving them a warning of something bad to come—death.

God explained to them about the tree and what it represented, but that wasn't enough. They needed to find out for themselves. Consequently, the combination of the devil, his lies, and their curiosity proved to be the deadly culmination. Take another look at your lives. Look at what God often gives you and others to do.

The picture is: He continues to entrust his children with his affairs. He will always give you opportunity through His mercy and grace. Try not to fail the Lord anymore. You can be in control with greater success, being aware that your flesh and the devil makes this deadly combination. However, we have no excuses. The Lord gives us a way to escape, and the power to resist anything that comes against us, when we do not want to be involved in it.

St. James 4: 7: "Submit yourselves therefore to God. Resist the devil, and he will flee from you." So, if you really want and need help from God to overcome any obstacles of weaknesses, the promise is here in the word. Just call on the Lord to deliver you!

We are given an opportunity for choice in obeying God and His commands. It's either obeying one master or the other. Which choice will you make? Let it be the right one, because the decision made by two people in the beginning of time had very devastating results for the world that we now live in. Making bad choices usually involves more than just one person, and everyone suffers.

In Adam and Eve's case, it involved the entire world and all humanity. What an impact! Can you imagine your choices having an impact like that? Well they do! Adam and Eve are not here to see the impact of their disobedience, but it's here. It is seen and felt by all of us throughout the world, and we're suffering from it.

Right now, there may be some things in your lives that have happened, and you're unable to see any or all of the damages done right now. You may not feel any hurt or pain, or no one may be suffering at this moment. However, it leaves scars that can't be erased. Once you're dead and gone, the *curiosity* or *your sin* could leave behind some serious repercussions. In any case, you would have done a considerable amount of destruction and damage, leaving an aftermath of mess. There is no other way to put it. It's just mess for you and others.

So through the obedience to God, we show that we love Him, and because we love, we fear Him as not to dissatisfy the Father. If we can stand on these principles and guidelines, we can all achieve our next level in the manifestations of abundant and prosperous living.

Again, in making the right choice to fear the Lord, we have confirmation to the existence of fear in the Lord. The word of God reassures us of the benefits and promises here in **Proverbs 14: 26-27:** "In the fear of the Lord *is* strong confidence: and his children shall have a place of refuge." **Verse 27:** "The fear of the Lord *is* a fountain of life, to depart from the snares of death."

Chapter VIII

Respect For God

Respect for God would be to show reverence toward Him. Reverence to God is the act of showing respect, giving esteem, honor, to give regard, or showing consideration. It's also a willingness to show appreciation. To show reverence for God signifies a feeling of profound awe with respect, and always, love. It is an act of being respectful and obedient. We need to always respect and show reverence to God and His sacred affairs.

Psalms 89: 7: "God is greatly to be feared in the assembly of the saints, and to be had in reverence of all *them that are* about him." I must say this and I do it with all due respect to my readers; I have to tell it like it is. We really do take God too lightly and for granted. What I mean is that God's word tells us how to conduct ourselves as saints of God at all times, as if we're in His presence.

There are those who have no respect. Their actions and conversations are foul, rude, and very ugly. We ride around with different types of religious emblems on our cars. We advertise our stance on God and try to witness to those who are on the streets about our love for Him and the love that He has to offer. Yet we are daring others and causing road rage, breaking every law and commandment there is.

Yes, people make us very angry. They act like they want to run us over and kill us. Some of them just don't care. We need to call on God in prayer for peace, to help us during times such as these. Our Father knows that we need prayer to sustain our flesh daily. We also purchase license plates to do our advertising and yet we don't yield to what they read or the statements claimed.

Be very careful, because sooner or later, there will be someone in back of you while you're in front of others who's allowed to see everything you do. When you advertise, people watch you. They really do. So please, be very conscientious about the things you say and do, because you never know who might be watching you.

We are stewards of God, representing Him and His cause. Sometimes the way we carry ourselves can cause someone to turn away, thus leaving a very bad taste in his or her mouth. We give and send out the wrong messages and signals. We make others afraid of what we have and that's not a good thing. Believe it or not, we are going to have to pay for those things.

Deuteronomy 14: 2: "For thou *art* an holy people unto the Lord thy God, and the Lord hath chosen thee to be a peculiar people unto himself, above all the nations that *are* upon the earth." We are to stand out and be different from the world because we are the salt of the earth. For the Lord said in **St. Matthew 5: 13:** "Ye are the salt of the earth: but if the salt have lost its savour, wherewith shall it be salted? It is thenceforth good for nothing, but to be cast out, and to be trodden under foot of men."

If we're in God and love Him, we will respect

Him to the highest. This brings forth respect for others. However, do not settle for being well-liked while handling situations as though the world would. The Lord will always fight your battle and make men respect you for who and what you are—*A child of the King,* the way He demands respect for Himself. Whereby, we are commissioned to make the world feel like…"Wow! I'd like to have what they have."

Chapter IX

Divine Delays While In Captivity

Deuteronomy 8: 2,3,5,6,17-20: "And thou shalt remember all the way which the Lord thy God led thee these forty years in the wilderness, to humble thee, *and* to prove thee, to know what *was* in thine heart, whether thou wouldest keep his commandments, or no."

Verse 3: "And he humbled thee, and suffered thee to hunger, and fed thee with manna, which thou knewest not, neither did thy fathers know; that he might make thee know that man doth not live by bread only, but by every *word* that proceedeth out of the mouth of the Lord doth man live."

Verse 5: "Thou shalt also consider in thine heart, that, as a man chasteneth his son, *so* the Lord thy God chasteneth thee."

Verse 6: "Therefore thou shalt keep the commandments of the Lord thy God, to walk in his ways, and to fear him."

Verse 17: "And thou say in thine heart, My power and the might of *mine* hand hath gotten me this wealth."

Verse 18: "But thou shalt remember the Lord thy God: for *it is* he that giveth thee power to get wealth, that he may establish his covenant which he sware unto thy fathers, as *it is* this day."

Verse 19: "And it shall be, if thou do at all forget the Lord thy God, and walk after other gods, and serve them, and worship them, I testify against you this day that ye shall surely perish."

Verse 20: "As the nations which the Lord destroyeth before your face, so shall ye perish; because ye would not be obedient unto the voice of the Lord your God."

Held Up

You're bound—life, finances, your mere existence as you know it, and everything surrounding you seems to be on hold. With all candor, and honesty to rob God sounds like a robbery...a "Hold Up!" When you're held captive, or in a hold up, you need to make the right decisions and move quickly. If God prompts you to move in your giving, you should do what He says. It is the right choice and you have to move immediately before you miss your blessings, and possibly fail your test.

"Held Up!" This could be in the giving of your tithes and offerings. To rob God of your tithes and offerings is very disturbing and disobedient, to say the least. When you hold up the kingdom of God and His work, you're actually holding up your own blessings and destiny. *You're bound!* Make a covenant with the Lord to give what He's asking.

Remember, it isn't yours anyway; it all belongs to Him. It's time to make the right decision. Will you allow the devil to continue to rob you of your blessings as you rob God? You must listen and obey God's word. Just remember it is God who gives you power to get wealth as the scripture stated. **Isaiah 55: 6:** "Seek ye the Lord while he may be found, call ye upon him while he is near:" **I Timothy 6: 17:** "Charge them that are rich in this world, that they be not highminded, nor trust in uncertain riches, but in the living God, who giveth us richly all things to enjoy;"

Giving is one way that pleases and will move God. Give out of your need to see what God will do for you. The scripture says "He will never leave you, or forsake you" and His word is so true! I'd like to share with you once again this precious information regarding one of the powers God has given you. It is in the tenth, or in the tithes,—and in Him is a God who can't, and will not lie. One sure way to get to your next level is in your giving.

To be blessed by God, you must keep His word and commandments. To give a portion back to God says *Thank you, Father,* and this honors God. He has and owns everything. We could never do anything that He couldn't do, or give back anything that He doesn't already have. Therefore, we should always obey His word. In expressing your love with admiration to the Father in worship, praise, and giving, you will always move Him to take you to the next level.

Your tithes and offerings play a beneficial part in your life. It will definitely be one of the determining factors in the outcome of your future. The giving of your tithes and offerings causes prosperity to come upon you and your family. This is due to the endowment of power from God for the increase. Therefore, do not just sit around waiting for God again to give you the wealth on a silver platter, although if He pleases He could do so.

It is only ten cents off of every dollar you've earned. That's not bad at all. There are some of you who blow that much or more before you get home after you get your paycheck. There are also times when you're in such a tight situation that you feel the need to keep it all just to make it. Now, let's be reasonable. Ten percent from every dollar is not going to make you, but it will eventually break you. I guarantee!

Now, in my spirit I know there are those of you who do not want to be in captivity with divine delays. So be obedient by keeping God's commandments as stated prior in **Deuternonomy 8: 6.** When you're obedient, the Lord takes a stand on His word and brings into fruition His promises.

Deuteronomy 8: 7-11: "For the Lord thy God bringeth thee into a good land, a land of brooks of water, of fountains and depths that spring out of valleys and hills;" **Verse 8:** "A land of wheat, and barley, and vines, and fig trees, and pomegranates; a land of oil olive, and honey;" **Verse 9:** "A land wherein thou shalt eat bread without scarceness, thou shalt not lack any *thing* in it; a land whose stones *are* iron, and out of whose hills thou mayest dig brass."

Keep in mind the requirements of God which are in the next verses.

Verse 10: "When thou hast eaten and art full, then thou shalt bless the Lord thy God for the good land which he hath given thee."

Verse 11: "Beware that thou forget not the Lord thy God, in not keeping his commandments, and his judgments, and his statutes, which I command thee this day:"

Debt Greater Than Your Credit

Nest Egg! How does this term make you feel? Does it make you feel all warm and fuzzy on the inside; wonderful, at ease, stable, and very comfortable? It takes away the feeling of worry and anxiety, doesn't it? You feel very confident in yourself, especially in the event of something going wrong in your life?

Savings account. I'm sure you're very familiar with the term. This one probably makes you feel content and safe as well. You have this to fall back on, just in case something comes up, such as emergencies, or to do a little something extra with your family, or perhaps just fulfill your heart's desire. If there is a need, you have the finances to do it. These are only a few of the reasons why you prepare yourself a nest egg in the first place or have a savings account.

Consequently, to trust in your feelings toward all these things is our nature. Having confidence in life because of your nest egg or savings is the *wrong answer*. You must have your confidence in "God only." He is the only source providing you with your money! Your finances are not the key or the source. God should be your nest egg; your source. Neither can you be covetous, holding on so tight with your finances. We need to relax and rely on Him at all times for everything, no matter what. Have you ever noticed that when we get a little something, it doesn't last long?

It seems to run through our fingers like sand in an hourglass. We need to invest more of our funds in God so He can multiply our dividends for a much greater harvest. Now, please don't misunderstand what I have just said here. The statement made is that there was nothing wrong in putting away to save. However, it is wrong to rely or trust in that savings and not in God, who is the source of the savings. It is also wrong to feel that because of my savings, my family and I will be fine. Although, it is right to feel that because of God, my family and I will be fine.

The minute we feel too confident is always the time when something goes wrong to subtract or take it away. Could I be right about this concept? I don't care how much you may have or can get your hands on; when you're not involving God, you are going to wind up with a debt larger than your credit. This is when things in your life can begin to take some incredible and drastic turns for the worse. You can be put into situations where you go through every single dime that you've saved. You may lose the money, misplace it, or just run out of it.

What good does it do to borrow money all the time when you find yourself back in the same situation, owing everyone? Forgive me for repeating some of the statements, but it's done purposely. I believe that when reading something or even saying it out loud, it tends to sink deeper within. Do you agree? So remember you cannot trust in yourselves, others, or your finances; you have to trust in God. If by chance you decided never to put another dime in a savings account or to have a nest egg, this should not make you feel any less confident than you were before, based on your faith.

Remember, never ever forget the incredible words that have so much meaning and power! These words have been put into a statement as a reminder to each and every one of you. The words themselves have such an awesome revelation of truth and can stand the test of time. These precious words—**In God We Trust**—are found on the back of all our money. Have you ever gotten that revelation and possibly thought who and why someone would put that statement on money? I believe that those words ring out a proclamation, proclaiming an official public announcement, a declaration, a formal statement, a solemn reminder, a serious oath.

Perhaps they knew about **I Timothy 6: 10:** "For the love of money is the root of all evil: which while some coveted after, they have erred from the faith, and pierced themselves through with many sorrows." I do believe without a shadow of doubt that this statement was meant as a reminder that we should not trust in money, but in God. This person must have known from experience that God is the one who will supernaturally and miraculously bring you out of any kind of situation, including financial woes. Therefore, trust in God and I guarantee, based on His word that He will make good on all of His promises.

The promise is that when your nest egg is God, it will never ever run out. He will always be there for you in your time of need and even for your desires. He will bless you so abundantly that you couldn't spend it all at once anyway. Let the Lord multiply your money for you, in order that you may live in abundance. You can be blessed or cursed. You see, some money has no power. It's the person with the money that has the power over it. If your money is good, clean, and backed by God, you live guilt free. You know that you have not robbed God, so you are free indeed!

Yes, we all need money. However, money without God is not good money. It is cursed money, uncertain money. When you give your tithes to God he doesn't keep your money; he multiplies it and increases it thirty, sixty, or a hundred fold.

These are the dividends depending on the ratio of your giving, as with a bank, only better. The more you put in, the more it multiplies. The difference is God's dividends are greater. Don't forget you can't beat God giving, but when you give, look to be advanced to another level in Christ in every area of your life. That's God's promise!

Hitting Rock Bottom

As Christians, we should not have to hit rock bottom. If you have gone that far, there is usually something wrong. There should be an explanation for what has happened in your lives. If you're honest, you'll usually find that through disobedience, not being consistent or persistent, your life will take a turn and wake you up!

That's why I'm writing this book. I'm here to help you not to make the same mistakes that I made. When the Holy Spirit prompts you to give or to do something, you need to move, or you will miss your blessing, the tide, or the wave. At that time things may be feasible and everything is right. Perhaps your nest egg is built up, and it seems very easy to give because it will not put a dent in your pocket.

So don't just sit on things waiting for the right time. This may have been the best time ever. While waiting for what we may call the right time, God may step in and allow a whirlwind of damage to affect you and your finances. When your nest egg doesn't have much because it has dwindled away, you begin to plunge into an area where your debt is greater than your credit. This is when you go into the mode of hitting rock bottom and finally it's a deeper plunge.

If you plan on coming out of that mode anytime soon, you'd better fall to your knees and ask God for forgiveness. Ask Him to show you how to come out of it and how to make a joyous comeback. I'll guarantee you that one of the ways to come back is through your giving. If you think about it, most of you may find that's where you went wrong. When you had it to give, you were being so stingy, and tight fisted, robbing God, when all the time you were really robbing yourself. Therefore, you fell short and deeper into the pit of having nothing left.

In trying to make this comeback, go to God and ask Him to help you make a fresh, new start. Ask for a clean slate. He will wipe away all of your debts. In modern day terms, we call it bankruptcy. Now it's time to ask God for a petition to file.

The Misfortune of Bankruptcy

Bankruptcy is not a joke or a game. It is nothing to play with. However, people in this day and time file bankruptcy like it's nothing at all. Therefore, the laws are slowly changing, making the process harder to do.

Bankruptcy interferes with your credit. It puts you in a bind to purchase and obtain things you desire in an honest and normal way. It allows sales people to take advantage of you because you've had some misfortune. They also take advantage of you because they know you are between a rock and a hard place.

If you try to purchase after bankruptcy, you will find that there are some who will not give you a fresh start. Most of the time you will accept anything they're offering because you don't have many choices. With the interest rates currently soaring through the roof, people want as much money as they can get from you. So this is the way it is for the next few years until the statue of limitations has expired. Bankruptcy, the process and procedure, can be a very, very traumatic experience.

What's worse is after the slate is cleared, when it's all nice and clean, most people do the exact same thing all over again. Same case scenario. File Bankruptcy With God. Let him wipe your slate clean. Allow Him to give you a fresh new start. However, this does not mean for you to repeat the same things over and over again.

I remember during a time in my life when things were bad and out of control. I decided I had to completely turn my finances over to God. I could not pay my bills and make it at the same time. I plunged so far downward because of my misfortune that I tried to hold on to every little bit that I had saved and kept for a rainy day.

There was the layoff on my job, then one thing after another. I felt as though I had no other choices. I needed help and no one could help me, only God. So I *filed* what some call **"Bankruptcy With God, And Not With Man."** Once I found another job, I started giving God my paychecks... (tithing). I would keep just enough money for gas to go to and from work, to church and back until the next pay period. I cut back on food, having just enough to get by.

As I stated, I couldn't pay any of my bills because I'd gotten so far behind. I was divorced and trying to raise my family all alone, which didn't help matters any. You name it and I was going through it. Now, let me tell you about someone. Hallelujah, praise God. Who can take a small amount of money, then multiply it so there is more than enough, more than when there were two providers or incomes. Some of you may be shocked and ask, "How is that possible? Isn't it better with two incomes?" The answer is yes! When both of you are serving the Lord it makes a big difference, when the believers are doers of the word and not hearers only. If you're not on one accord with your finances in giving and standing on the word of God, it is not going to work. There will be hardship.

People often believe that if their spouse hadn't left, things might have turned out differently or even better for them. Although I remember struggling with the both of us. At the time, we made a whole lot more together than I made by myself. However, when you trust in God and you're alone, He will supernaturally make it all work out. God is so incredible; faithful and true to His word.

I can tell you from personal experience, when I began to give my tithe and seed offerings, consistently, I watched God turn my life and my finances completely around. I had to give out of need because I felt if anyone could do something about my situation it surely would be God. I was not in the mood, nor could I afford to try and figure out who was going to get paid. After I put my life completely and totally in God's hands, my life began to change and I've never been the same since.

"Money Cometh" became my motto, the words most commonly used around my church. Consequently it came to pass. It came from every direction of the North, South, East, and the West. My financial blessings started the same day I stepped out of the boat. I started to keep my eyes fixed on God and not on my situation. This was the day that I began to walk on the water and trust in God. There was increase from every area (people, places and things). My life began slowly getting back on track.

Getting there slowly was a good thing because God was rebuilding a stronger, much better foundation in my faith and my life. I'm better off now than ever before because of the realization and a closer relationship with God. He means business! If the Lord needs to, He will break you down into tiny little pieces to rebuild and start you all over again. Don't take it personally, though; it's all for the making of a better you because He loves you that much.

Many of you might say, "If you hadn't got laid off this would never have happened." No matter what happens or how the money may fall short due to unexpected reasons, just continue to be faithful to the Lord. The reason doesn't matter. Give God what is due to Him right off the very top and He will never fail you. If you feel things are working out just fine without your obedience to the word, just give it some time; it won't last.

Look at it this way: you can only drive your car for so long without gas, water, oil, coolant, etc. Eventually it is going to stop. It's the same way with God. You can only go so long without Him in your life and your affairs. Eventually you are going to suffer. You're going to need Him and you will call on His name one day.

Now I know there are just a few of you out there who can identify with what I'm saying. Please share with others to help them know the truth. Let them know who is really behind a *great success*. The devil will always try to deceive you and make you feel that your great success is all by your own power and might. That is so far from being the truth; eventually you will suffer a great penalty because of your small way of thinking.

Chapter X

Chastisement And Abasement

Deuteronomy 8: 5: "Thou shalt also consider in thine heart, that, as a man chasteneth his son, so the Lord thy God chasteneth thee." The Lord chastises you because He loves you, just as a good father who loves his child would. When a solid, strong father reprimands his child for doing wrong, there is usually a *going through* process during this period. In combination with it, there is also a testing period where there is a taking away of things, being without, going through, affliction, penalty, and many more scenarios just to make sure you will never forget and always remember to obey.

The main objective in discipline or chastisement is to educate, give structure, mold, make, renew, test, or convey to a single person, or perhaps a group of people, that you mean business and you mean what you say!

In looking into an adult's life regarding chastisement and abasement, we need to take it on a much deeper level. In our society, these methods are sometimes just not enough to get the point across. For example, the world crisis that took place on September 11, 2001 would be an extreme case scenario. However, because of this incident, to do anything against the law, rules, or regulations of any governing factor, you will have to pay even a greater penalty. This could also mean doing anything against God, a parent, or law enforcement. The person or persons responsible would have to pay. There would be chastising, reprimanding, or punishment to the fullest extent.

In some extreme cases, others may have to pay even if innocent, just to get the point across that you mean business. Now would you honor, esteem, spoil, or make very comfortable those not obeying or adhering to the commandments, laws, rules, and regulations? With another perspective look again at **Deuteronomy 8: 2-3,6:** "And thou shalt remember all the way which the Lord thy God led thee these forty years in the wilderness, to humble thee, *and* to prove thee, to know what *was* in thine heart, whether thou wouldest keep his commandments, or no."

Verse 3: "And he humbled thee, and suffered thee to hunger, and fed thee with manna, which thou knewest not, neither did thy fathers know; that he might make thee know that man doth not live by bread only, but by every *word* that proceedeth out of the mouth of the Lord doth man live."

Now once the initial chastising has begun, you are taken away and put into a holding or isolated area. During the chastisement, you are generally held in captivity, depending on the level or nature of being disobedient. **Verse 6:** "Therefore thou shalt keep the commandments of the Lord thy God, to walk in his ways, and to fear him."

To sum it all up, we have to realize the importance of the chastisement and the crucial message learned. During the consistency of being in captivity, we really should have learned a valuable lesson and received the information and the validity of it, being able to make much better decisions and/or choices in our own lives.

If you receive the information, take the message to heart, get it deep within your spirit, then you will begin to obey God. It is clear that when you accept and take full responsibility for your actions, the chastisement can be lifted and the reproofing can begin.

God the Father, the parent, or the law, then removes the child, person, or group of people out of its captivity. Whoever is overseeing the situation as he or she begin to feel that adequate results have been accomplished to warrant a dismissal of the punishment depending on its severity, will dismiss the punishment. Often following is a series of questions or test. This will determine and confirm the results of the reproofing. The decision made will be based on the results confirming that the lesson has been well-received and that the person or persons hereby acknowledge what has been taught. There's full recompense and therefore they may be released on their own recognizance.

However, if your stance on all of this information was not to conform, then your heart was hardened. Therefore, you will continue to trust in self, others, or your finances. Then as painfully as it may sound, the lesson learned here is the: "wrong answer, the wrong answer, the wrong answer."

Deuteronomy 8: 12-17: "Lest when thou hast eaten and art full, and hast built goodly houses, and dwelt therein;" **Verse 13:** "And *when* thy herds and thy flocks multiply, and thy silver and thy gold is multiplied, and all that thou hast is multiplied;"

Verse 14: "Then thine heart be lifted up, and thou forget the Lord thy God, which brought thee forth out of the land of Egypt, from the house of bondage;" **Verse 15:** "Who led thee through that great and terrible wilderness, *wherein were* fiery serpents, and scorpions, and drought, where *there was* no water; who brought thee forth water out of the rock of flint;" **Verse 16:** "Who fed thee in the wilderness with manna, which thy fathers knew not, that he might humble thee, and that he might prove thee, to do thee good at thy latter end;"

Verse 17: "And thou say in thine heart, My power and the might of *mine* hand hath gotten me this wealth." Pay close attention to the last verse, because thinking in the manner is surely the wrong answer and definitely has its repercussions. We have to be careful not to exalt ourselves, or get puffed up, arrogant, prideful, or haughty.

Proverbs 16: 18: "Pride goeth before destruction, and an haughty spirit before a fall." Your life is not worth this fall. **Proverbs 16: 16:** "How much better *is it* to get wisdom than gold! and to get understanding rather to be chosen than silver!" **Proverbs 16: 19-20:** "Better *it is* to be of an humble spirit with the lowly, than to divide the spoil with the proud."

Verse 20: "He that handleth a matter wisely shall find good: and whoso trusteth in the Lord, happy *is* he."

Let's also take another glimpse at the title and question of the author's first book. "*TRUSTING GOD?*...self, others or finances?" **Proverbs 29: 23:** "A man's pride shall bring him low: but honour shall uphold the humble in spirit." With this being a very high penalty to pay, does abasement sound like something you'd enjoy and would be most proud and happy to go through with?

Let's continue through the word of God. **I Corinthians 4: 18-20:** "Now some are puffed up as though I would not come to you." **Verse 19:** "But I will come to you shortly, if the Lord will, and will know, not the speech of them which are puffed up, but the power." **Verse 20:** "For the kingdom of God *is* not in word, but in power."

Proverbs 11: 2: "*When* pride cometh, then cometh shame: but with the lowly *is* wisdom." To bring all of this a little closer to home, I will test your spirit with a very simple question.

Who wants to continue to refuse instruction from our Father regarding His business to be brought low with your head hung down in shame and disgrace knowing that everyone knows, and can see that you've come to ruin? **Proverbs 13: 18:** "Poverty and shame *shall be to* him that refuseth instruction: but he that regardeth reproof shall be honoured."

Chapter XI

Refining And Reproofing

The act of refining is the removal of unwanted matter; to polish and make pure. When we cultivate or make a change, add or extend to improve someone or something, this would also be an act of refining.

After one has gone through chastisement and abasement, we can't assume that the particular act done by that person will not be repeated. We need to ensure that this person has grown, matured in knowledge and wisdom. Now, are they ready for the next level of faith by God or lesson by their superiors? There has to be a refining period, a time of putting away all of the old things and ways.

II Corinthians 5: 17: "Therefore if any man *be* in Christ, *he is* a new creature: old things are passed away; behold, all things are become new." Receiving Christ in your life or being renewed means that you're cleansed and freed in your spirit of all impurities. There is also chastisement and correction. If that is not getting to the root of the problem, then there has definitely been a hardening of the heart and their ways. Then abasement is surely the next step!

Once this has been achieved we come back again

to the potter. This is where God is the potter and we are the clay. **Jeremiah 18: 1-6:** "The word which came to Jeremiah from the Lord, saying," **Verse 2:** "Arise, and go down to the potter's house, and there I will cause thee to hear my words." **Verse 3:** "Then I went down to the potter's house, and, behold, he wrought a work on the wheels." **Verse 4:** "And the vessel that he made of clay was marred in the hand of the potter: so he made it again another vessel, as seemed good to the potter to make *it*." **Verse 5:** "Then the word of the Lord came to me, saying," **Verse 6:** "O house of Israel, cannot I do with you as this potter? saith the Lord. Behold, as the clay *is* in the potter's hand, so *are* ye in mine hand, O house of Israel."

God is our divine teacher and He has divine control. All He asks is for repentance in being disobedient to His word, unlike any parent, law enforcer, or rule regulator, when we are at the mercy of their hands and they can do what they please. They can reform, remake, or remold us to be exactly what they want us to be if done in the proper manner. That's where the refining comes along. **Job 23: 10:** "But he knoweth the way that I take: *when* he hath tried me, I shall come forth as gold." **Isaiah 48: 10:** "Behold, I have refined thee, but not with silver; I have chosen thee in the furnace of affliction."

Malachi 3: 3: "And he shall sit *as* a refiner and purifier of silver: and he shall purify the sons of Levi, and purge them as gold and silver, that they may offer unto the Lord an offering in righteousness."

I Peter 1: 7: "That the trial of your faith, being much more precious than of gold that perisheth, though it be tried with fire, might be found unto praise and honour and glory at the appearing of Jesus Christ:" **I Peter 4: 12:** "Beloved, think it not strange concerning the fiery trial which is to try you, as though some strange thing happened unto you:" Now, let's go back again to **Deuteronomy 8: 2:** "And thou shalt remember all the way which the Lord thy God led thee these forty years in the wilderness, to humble thee, *and* to prove thee, to know what *was* in thine heart, whether thou wouldest keep his commandments, or no." To reprove, convict, or rebuke is the act of testing or checking the validity of something or someone to make a decision, prove, convince, or to judge.

Proverbs 12: 1: "Whoso loveth instruction loveth knowledge: but he that hateth reproof *is* brutish." **Proverbs 15: 10:** "Correction *is* grievous unto him that forsaketh the way: *and* he that hateth reproof shall die." **Proverbs 15: 31-32:** "The ear that heareth the reproof of life abideth among the wise." **Verse 32:** "He that refuseth instruction despiseth his own soul: but he that heareth reproof getteth understanding."

Also read **Proverbs 29: 15-17:** "The rod and reproof give wisdom: but a child left to *himself* bringeth his mother to shame." **Verse 16:** "When the wicked are multiplied, transgression increaseth: but the righteous shall see their fall." **Verse 17:** "Correct thy son, and he shall give thee rest; yea, he shall give delight unto thy soul."

There are times in our lives when we need to be corrected. For the Lord, or a father or mother to turn their back on the wrong you've done could be a very costly decision. For them to turn their back on you, in your opinion, wouldn't show any love.

Its reason is one that is of love that we chastise and use the rod of correction because it reproves us. It brings about wisdom, knowledge, and the understanding that we need in our lives to help guide us along the way. Tell me, who really loves a child and leaves him to stumble?

Proverbs 13: 24: "He that spareth his rod hateth his son: but he that loveth him chasteneth him betimes." It doesn't matter how many times it takes to get it right; God does not and will not hate you. I just can't say it enough; God loves you. Can't you see that?

He proved His love, but He didn't just stop there. Once again, He gave His only son to die for us to save us from our sins. What love the Father has for His sons and daughters, His children, His heirs. **I Corinthians 4: 20-21:** "For the kingdom of God *is* not in word, but in power." **Verse 21:** "What will ye? shall I come unto you with a rod, or in love, and *in* the spirit of meekness?" Another question for you is: "What would you rather have?"

Chapter XII

Throne Of Mercy And The Pillar Of Grace

Mercy and Grace, as some would say, the twins, is a pair that works together hand in hand. The qualities and characteristics are relatively similar. Mercy bestows feelings of kindness, goodwill, compassion, and sympathy. Grace introduces and presents favorable regards, graciousness, loving kindness, goodwill, and most of all, divine favor. With regards to sin, the expiation, the act of atoning was necessary and consistent with God's holiness and for His righteous sake.

His grace, love, and mercy have provided the atonement in the sacrificing of His son. Being sinners brings justification to be being exposed to the wrath of God. The hostility is not on the part of God; it is on the part of man. Through the accomplishment of Christ, through His death, man escapes the merited wrath of God, so often seen and felt through the undaunted love, mercy, and grace of our Lord and Savior Jesus Christ.

Mercy

Mercy, being the most common to us, could mean the act of kindness from someone of power for someone in distress. Clemency: a fortunate act or occurrence; a blessing. However, another term used could be: "at the mercy of" (in the hands of someone or something that has power over you). Mercy could also be an outward manifestation of pity or a sorrowful feeling. It assumes need on the part of the one who receives it, and the resources adequate to meet the need on the part of the one who shows it. God, who is rich in mercy, uses it.

Ephesians 2: 4: "But God, who is rich in mercy, for his great love wherewith he loved us,"

St. Luke 1: 50: "And his mercy *is* on them that fear him from generation to generation." **Titus 3: 5:** "Not by works of righteousness which we have done, but according to his mercy he saved us, by the washing of regeneration, and renewing of the Holy Ghost;"

St. Luke 1: 72: "To perform the mercy *promised* to our fathers, and to remember his holy covenant;" **I Timothy 1: 16:** "Howbeit for this cause I obtained mercy, that in me first Jesus Christ might shew forth all longsuffering, for a pattern to them which should hereafter believe on him to life everlasting."

Now, let's take some time to ponder the last request that God asked of you. Have you completed it yet? When do you think you might feel like doing it? When will you take time out of your busy schedule and complicated life to complete the task? Have you ever stopped to think what if God handled our affairs the way we do His in this same slothful manner? Some of us would be in very bad shape. There are a few of you who just do nothing and will never follow the Lord's command.

Also, there are some of those who do so only when it is convenient. What if God was never on time, not meeting our needs, nor giving of our heart's desires? No healing of our bodies, no devouring of the enemy, not anything. What if He was never there to protect us from our own mess ups? The list could go on. Even though we disappoint the Lord over and over again, He continues to show us endless mercy and love. He still stands on His word, and never changes His mind. It doesn't matter what we do, He is true to His word and keeps all of His promises.

There will come a time when the mercy of the Lord is so needed in your life, when minor things bind, block, and stop your movements. When you're on a mission for the Lord and you get blocked, just know that it is the work of the enemy and he comes in many forms to kill, steal, and to destroy. Don't let the enemy get over on you. You need to pray, pray, and then pray some more. Hold on and call on the name of the Lord. Plead the blood of Jesus if you have to.

You see, Christ is about our business. He does not half-step regarding anything He has to do for us. So why should we?

If you get it right the first time, you will not have to use His mercies for being disobedient when something is asked of you. Don't get me wrong; His mercy is a good thing. I thank God for it because there are times I need it. If mercy is needed, let it not have to be because of your disobedience.

You see, I fear my Father and reverence Him. So I have to make sure my heart is right at all times regarding my desire for Him because it must not be slack. He is my life, my source, my joy, my all and all. When you're trying so very hard, doesn't it just break your heart when you don't do what you're supposed to do? If it's the distraction, just pray to remove yourself or whatever it is that is distracting you. Nothing satisfies me more than to do the Lord's work at this time in my life. He is priority on my list, and you know how we feel when it seems as though He has forgotten all about us. We're hurt when we feel that we are not priority in His affairs or when it seems as though He has turned a deaf ear.

Just remember, we have to give in to the Lord's affairs to receive blessings of the Lord as well. So the question still remains, why should we use up the mercies when it is not necessary? It doesn't take much to please God. All He wants is your love and obedience to His word and commandments.

So let's get it together, my sisters and brothers in the Lord, and also those of you who have not made a commitment to the Lord, to make Him your Savior. Let's try to get on one accord and get about our Father's business. Just keep in mind, in the realm of obedience, you will not have to use His mercies. Just love the Lord and do His will. You will be greatly rewarded by Him. It makes me content to see my Father happy because I love Him so much. However, if His mercy is ever needed, just remember an all-time favorite scripture found in **I Chronicles 16: 34:** "Oh give thanks unto the Lord; for *he is* good; for his mercy *endureth* for ever."

Grace

Grace, as I said before, falls under the category of goodwill, divine favor, and mercy. In the case of God's redemptive mercy and grace, the pleasure it gives Him for the recipient is sometimes set in contrast with debt, works, the law, etc. On the part of the receiver, a sense of the favor bestowed is a feeling of gratitude and thankfulness. God will bestow upon you unmerited favor and grace along with His kindness and mercy. Tell me, what is it that you have now that could merit so much more than that?

All of these things follow from humbling yourselves and turning away from the world. God alone is the giving source of such undeserved favor. He is asked repeatedly for such gracious acts only He can do. Another one of my favorites is: **II Corinthians 12: 9:** "And he said unto me, My grace is sufficient for thee: for my strength is made perfect in weakness." Thank God for His grace! I think all would agree and say,Amen! **I Peter 5: 10:** "But the God of all grace, who hath called us unto his eternal glory by Christ Jesus, after that ye have suffered a while, make you perfect, stablish, strengthen, settle *you*."

Also, God's grace is freely given to all men. It empowers men for service. It is also promised to the humbled. Accordingly to **Acts 15: 11:** "But we believe that through the grace of the Lord Jesus Christ we shall be saved, even as they."
Romans 3: 24: "Being justified freely by his grace through the redemption that is in Christ Jesus:"

Let's take a look at yet another scripture and let this one move in your spirit.

II Corinthians 8: 9: "For ye know the grace of our Lord Jesus Christ, that, though he was rich, yet for your sakes he became poor, that ye through his poverty might be rich." Do you realize what that scripture should mean to us? He has made His grace sufficient for all of us and to prove it, look at **II Corinthians 12: 9:** "And he said unto me, My grace is sufficient for thee: for my strength is made perfect in weakness. Most gladly therefore will I rather glory in my infirmities, that the power of Christ may rest upon me." Can we beat that with man? No. Man cannot offer you grace. This is the wrong answer. God's grace is free and given to all men only by Him.

Romans 5: 15: "But not as the offence, so also *is* the free gift. For if through the offence of one many be dead, much more the grace of God, and the gift by grace, *which is* by one man, Jesus Christ, hath abounded unto many." **Ephesians 1: 7:** "In whom we have redemption through his blood, the forgiveness of sins, according to the riches of his grace;" **Ephesians 2: 7:** "That in the ages to come he might shew the exceeding riches of his grace in *his* kindness toward us through Christ Jesus."

I Timothy 1: 14: "And the grace of our Lord was exceeding abundant with faith and love which is in Christ Jesus." **Titus 2: 11:** "For the grace of God that bringeth salvation hath appeared to all men."**Titus 3:7:** "That being justified by his grace, we should be made heirs according to the hope of eternal life."

Let's look at one more scripture in **Romans 4: 16:** "Therefore *it is* of faith, that *it might be* by grace; to the end the promise might be sure to all the seed; not to that only which is of the law, but to that also which is of the faith of Abraham; who is the father of us all." Now regarding the mercies and grace of God, I'd like to add that we should all show more gratitude to our Father, who is so gracious to us in freely giving of all of the unmerited favor. One way we can do this is by praising God for His goodness.

We can do it in song, worship, prayer, supplication, musical instruments, obedience, etc. It should be universal. **Psalms 67: 3:** "Let the people praise thee, O God; let all the people praise thee." **Isaiah 42: 12:** "Let them give glory unto the Lord, and declare his praise in the islands." Our praise and thankfulness should be perpetual, lasting forever, continuous, and indefinite.

Hebrews 13: 15: "By him therefore let us offer the sacrifice of praise to God continually, that is, the fruit of *our* lips giving thanks to his name." Hold steadfast to your heart that we as a people, as a whole, have a four-fold reason and it is found in **I Peter 2: 9:** "But ye are a chosen generation, a royal priesthood, an holy nation, a peculiar people; that ye should shew forth the praises of him who hath called you out of darkness into his marvellous light."

Chapter XIII

Renewing Your Covenant

To renew means to start over again, to set up, to recreate. To securely set into position, a condition in this case, a covenant with God. A covenant could be a pact, a vow, an oath, a binding agreement, contract, pledge, or a promise made by two or more persons or parties. **Ephesians 5: 15:** "See then that ye walk circumspectly, not as fools, but as wise." Don't be foolish about the things concerning God. Our vows, the agreements or whatever the case may be, have to be kept very sacred between you and God.

Ecclesiastes 5: 4: "When thou vowest a vow unto God, defer not to pay it; for *he hath* no pleasure in fools: pay that which thou hast vowed." **Numbers 30: 2:** "If a man vow a vow unto the Lord, or swear an oath to bind his soul with a bond; he shall not break his word, he shall do according to all that proceedeth out of his mouth."

To reiterate, one of my downfalls was because of this very same scenario. After being blessed, God took me to another level. Things were not tight and somewhat good. What God asked me to do turned out to be a vow that would have been easily made and satisfied, if only I would have moved immediately and been obedient. As time went on, I waited for the right time. That time never came. As a matter of fact, things began to fall apart and get real bad, hitting "rock bottom."

The small stash that I had went right through my fingers and forget about that nest egg, it was here today and gone tomorrow. No one can tell me any different; it's like night and day when you move, once God directs you as to what to do. God knew those circumstances were coming. But He tried to prepare me by increasing my holdings. While holding on so tight I lost that, plus a lot more. Now I've learned to take His tithe right off the top, no matter what the circumstances are. Don't just stand there weighing your options, because the storm can hit so fast that you don't have time to get another answer, other than what God has already told you.

There is no reason to make the same mistakes. Doing this spells failure over and over again. How many times have we been in big trouble and man could not help in the situation? Things were so bad that you had to call on the name of the Lord. Even the non-believer. When things get rough and you get in a pinch, you always know how to say or call on the name, "Jesus."

For some reason, you call on the name of Jesus because you know that deep down inside He is who He says He is. Also some of you have been on your sick bed and didn't want to die and were fearful. As a last resort, to escape pain or death, you began to pray and make promises to the Lord.

I can just hear some of you when no one is around, or in the wee hours of the night, calling on the Lord, just pleading for His help. Well, continue to read the scriptures and remember not to break your covenant, your bond or your word, because the Lord takes you at your word.

The more I've gone through, the more I've grown in the Lord and it's more evident than ever that the mercy and grace of God have surrounded me. Because of this very reason, it's more evident and real than ever before. As time has progressed, and I have developed a very close and tight knit bond with the Lord, I'm more concerned about my vows, promises, and my commitments. You have to fear God and reverence the Holy Spirit. You need to really love God and respect what comes out of your mouth to Him.

Sometimes we use it to get what we want and need. Sometimes we pray, "Oh Lord, if you only do this, then I'll do this, and this, I promise. Just help me to get out of this. Heal me of this." Or "We really need that;" the list goes on. Does this sound familiar to you? Now, I'm not talking about people who are really, really trying and desperately mean it from the heart. God knows your heart and that is what He weighs. Keep that in mind.

Deuteronomy 23: 21: "When thou shalt vow a vow unto the Lord thy God, thou shalt not slack to pay it: for the Lord thy God will surely require it of thee; and it would be sin in thee." Did you know that scripture was in the Bible? I know there are just a few who didn't and if I could help at least one soul survive the wrath of God, then so be it. Now that you know, your life will be changed as of right now. There will be a new beginning, a new start. A new leaf just turned over in your life and now maybe you can go to a new level with Christ. Now you know that you have to be a little more serious and cautious about the affairs of the Lord.

Renewing your covenant with God, recapping based on the scripture **Deuteronomy 8**, comes with chastising if you remember in the previous chapter. This portion comes first. Once that point is well taken, then the Lord our God, reaffirms the same covenant again with you. **Deuteronomy 8: 6:** "Therefore thou shalt keep the commandments of the Lord thy God, to walk in his ways, and to fear him." Once we have begun to keep His word, we can then stand on some strong promises, such as **Deuteronomy 8: 7-9.** To paraphrase these three promises that I've mentioned in previous chapters, the Lord God says He will bring you into a good land, a land without scarceness and thou shalt not lack anything. What a glorious promise. Now let's review.

Deuteronomy 8: 18: "But thou shalt remember the Lord thy God: for *it is* he that giveth thee power to get wealth, that he may establish his covenant which he sware unto thy fathers, as *it is* this day." So, God is saying let's give this thing another try based on His endless love, kindness, grace, and mercy. So love thy Father as He loves us, with all of your heart, mind, body, and soul. Form with Christ a very personal, intimate relationship. Bond with Him in all you do, no matter how small or how frivolous it may seem. You must acknowledge God in all things and He will surely direct your path.

Chapter XIV

Your Atonement

This will be simple and made very easy. Your atonement is the blood of Jesus shed for us through His death, burial, and resurrection. Through this sacrifice, our sin has been wiped away, purged, and forgiven. Reconciliation and propitiation could also mean the "Mercy seat of God" by which He shows mercy to all sinners. When Christ forgives us, it means that we are washed as white as snow. Our sins are never to be remembered, scattered further than the east is from the west and the north is from the south.

God loves you. He sent forth His Son to die so that we might have the right to the tree of life. It's His blood that cleanses us and gives us life. So we are covered by the blood of Jesus and there are three short steps to take advantage of this wonderful *Gift*.

I call them the ABC's of life:

A) Admit: For all have sinned and come short of the glory of God.

B) Believe: That God sent forth His Son to die on the cross to save you from sin and destruction.

C) Confess: With thy mouth the Lord Jesus, and believe in thine heart that God hath raised Him from the dead, thou shalt be saved.

This is a very simple form of restoration to renew or reconfirm your relationship with the Father. Don't miss out another day; just try it. You won't regret one day with the Father, for He is and He will complete you.

If you feel that you have everything you could possibly ever want and yet there is still an emptiness, God can and will complete you. If you're empty and don't know where to go or where to turn, you need Jesus. He will complete you. If all else fails, and the majority of the time it has always been failing, just call on Jesus, for He will answer your prayers.

Sometimes we rely on quick fixes. We have to spend money for happiness. We have to busy ourselves so much that it overcomes the loneliness and sadness in our lives. We've become workaholics to wipe out fears and stages of loneliness. All you really need is Jesus. He is so big that He can fill the void of emptiness. Just give Him a try. He is the only one who can complete you. God will never change. Just remember God loves you!

Chapter XV

Abundant And Prosperous Living

God wants us to live fruitfully, abundantly, and full of prosperity through Jesus Christ. However, there is something we must do as His people. **St. Matthew 6: 33:** "But seek ye first the kingdom of God, and his righteousness; and all these things shall be added unto you." **Psalms 37: 4:** "Delight thyself also in the Lord; and he shall give thee the desires of thine heart."

Believe, confess, and stand on those scriptures every single day. It truly works! You must meditate on the word every day to get it deep down on the inside. You have to feel it within. When there are times of negativity by anyone or anything, you can stand still, firm, and tall saying, I know—that I know—that I know, and nothing or no one can do anything to change that!

Do this daily and you will see a big difference in your life with fruitful results. This helps you in your faith, to take hold, getting a grip on you and your life. By doing this, God really moves when your faith is stirred up, when He can see it operating. Believe me, it really works. You should also watch what you speak forth. As you know, you can speak negative things into existence in your life. If you don't have anything positive to say, don't say anything at all.

Don't put yourself in a position to fail. Place yourselves in the midst of *multipliers,* not *subtractors*. Surround yourself with people who have a personal relationship with God, who really love and reverence Him. Be in the midst of people who are standing firm, stepping out on faith, seeking deeper depths and higher heights in the Lord. In doing this you will gain knowledge, wisdom, and strength.

Don't find yourself surrounded by the kind of people and things that bring you down making you want to take back your stance with God. Separate yourself from those who always have a negative connotation about the Lord and His work. One of the largest and most deceitful allegations that the devil tries to infiltrate into the minds of people is that they never need to go to church. This being used as a scapegoat is one of the biggest lies ever told. It's not only about praying a couple of lines daily out loud, or in your heart, for that matter. It's about needing the word of God to sustain you. You need someone in authority having the knowledge, wisdom, and understanding of being able to lead, guide, and teach you. We're like cars; we need to be filled up from time to time using premium; it's the best. The true word of God! You also need the fellowship of other believers for accountability. There is condemnation regarding your conscience when the word of God is being taught in a structured setting. There are times you'll need encouragement and to be *lifted up,* which is your *tune-up*! This is very important to continue to run well.

Hebrews 10: 25-26: "Not forsaking the assembling of ourselves together, as the manner of some *is;* but exhorting *one another*: and so much the more, as ye see the day approaching." This admonition involves more than your church attendance and being in a sanctuary. It involves the entire worship of Christ without neglect of duty. It provides encouragement, strength, lifting up one to another and the stirring up from the worship and the fellowship.

Verse 26: "For if we sin willfully after that we have received the knowledge of the truth, there remaineth no more sacrifice for sins." If your choice is not to go somewhere because you feel you can get it all at home alone with no studying, no structure or guidelines, then you are kidding yourself, and misleading others. When you assemble yourselves with other children of God, hearing the teaching of His word, you receive more strength.

St. Matthew 18: 20: "For where two or three are gathered together in my name, there am I in the midst of them." Strength comes in numbers. Two or three with Jesus in the midst makes a powerful circle, making the devil tremble. You have protection; you're less vulnerable, and weak. There is always someone to help you or pick you up if you should fall.

Due to the fact that we can't see God, we don't worry about a lot of things that we may do or say. Therefore, when it comes to a physical being that we can see and touch, that we're having to give an account to, we seem to care more about our sins in most cases. However, the closer we get to the Lord, our condemnation arouses based solely on the love we have for Him. We fall down with our faces in shame, shedding our tears because we don't want to hurt our Father. When we stay away, forsaking the church, not getting the word deep down on the inside, we tend to lose that. Once it's gone, we begin to die out, becoming lifeless with no real meaning, sense of value, or worth to anyone.

Don't let the devil lie to you and cheat you anymore! When God's word gets deep down on the inside, it comes alive and gives you strength. The devil can only work with a weak vessel toying with its mind and heart. Unfortunately, this can happen when you're weak, having nothing to fight back with. For example: you don't expect your car to run smoothly mile after mile without its checkup. You cannot neglect giving your vehicle what it needs to run smoothly and safely.

As previously said, we need tune-ups. We need our oil changed every so many miles. We need to be filled up with the right things to make it through to the following week. In remembering not to forsake the assembling of yourselves, just come on in as if you were taking your car to get it worked on for same day service. Come right on down to the house of God to get yourselves in working condition. This is where you come for a free diagnostic test to get all the kinks worked out. If needed, you can have surgery done, and be rehabilitated all in the same breath. Look at God! He is so awesome!

When you're constantly on the battlefield being attacked by the enemy, you have more power backed by the body of Christ. You have more strength, which builds your faith, giving you what you need, or what you may be seeking. When you do not read your Bibles, thus not getting the word deep on the inside to know what to stand on, it doesn't give you any weapons to fight with. Believe me—this is the time he'll really try to get next to you.

Likewise, we must back the body of Christ. We must honor our ministry. Yielding to give for its growth and development, helping others come to know Christ. Besides, do you realize that Christ is not coming back until His word is a witness to all nations? We have a lot of work cut out for us to do. **St. Matthews 24: 14:** "And this gospel of the kingdom shall be preached in all the world for a witness unto all nations; and then shall the end come."

Wouldn't you like to play a part in sowing into someone's life? Therefore, don't refuse to give into the ministries. We are always held accountable for our own hearts and what we do. We should not care about what others do. Our intentions, when we give, should always be good because we are helping others not to lose out. Don't worry about things that you can't change or do anything about.

Only God has the power to ensure that others will get what is indeed intended for them. It doesn't matter what others have done, and who they've done it to. If others don't obey and do what God has told them to do with what has been given them, then that's on them, not you. You only have to give an account for what you do. We need to pray, and forgive so we can be forgiven, allowing God to do his job. Let the Lord lead you in what, how, and when you should give.

Remember, you're not giving to man, it's unto God. Acknowledge the request with an excitement during your obedience with a cheerful heart, not grudgingly; giving in love from your heart because this is what matters. Being obedient to the Lord makes you feel well in your soul.

When you give your portion that is due to the Lord, which is totally the word and a strong requirement of God, making money works on any amount given to the Kingdom of God. I consider God as the source; my bank of heaven. I give my tithes and gift offerings to God and He stores it in the bank of heaven to multiply my seed sown.

Can you ever imagine some thirty, sixty, or a hundred-fold? Your giving is compounded daily at a very high interest rate. You can't beat those rates of return that you receive anywhere. Only ten percent of your earnings produces dividends unlike any bank has ever done before.

My thought is that ten percent is really not a lot of money if you don't need it. However, if you're investing in a bank, they are now requesting a portion of that money just to open and sustain an account for you, when only yesterday it was twenty-five dollars or less to open any type of checking or savings. God doesn't do this. He invests one hundred percent of all your funds.

This is another excellent reason to give God's portion back to Him. In some cases the returns start almost immediately. I've found that as soon as the money leaves your hand, God has another blessing in store and it's already on the way. When the Lord lays upon your heart to bless or give in a specific way, just be obedient and never think twice. The Lord promises that the more you give, the more you receive. Don't worry about what you haven't done in the past.

Start now to get things right with the Lord. Start today giving God what's due to Him faithfully and consistently. That is the only way that it will work.

Deuteronomy 28: 1-14: "And it shall come to pass, if thou shalt hearken diligently unto the voice of the Lord thy God, to observe *and* to do all his commandments which I command thee this day, that the Lord thy God will set thee on high above all nations of the earth:" **Verse 2:** "And all these blessings shall come on thee, and overtake thee, if thou shalt hearken unto the voice of the Lord thy God."

Verse 3: "Blessed *shalt* thou *be* in the city, and blessed *shalt* thou *be* in the field." **Verse 4:** "Blessed *shall be* the fruit of thy body, and the fruit of thy ground, and the fruit of thy cattle, the increase of thy kine, and the flocks of thy sheep." **Verse 5:** "Blessed *shall be* thy basket and thy store." **Verse 6:** "Blessed *shalt* thou *be* when thou comest in, and blessed *shalt* thou *be* when thou goest out." **Verse 7:** "The Lord shall cause thine enemies that rise up against thee to be smitten before thy face: they shall come out against thee one way, and flee before thee seven ways."

Verse 8: "The Lord shall command the blessing upon thee in thy storehouses, and in all that thou settest thine hand unto; and he shall bless thee in the land which the Lord thy God giveth thee." **Verse 9:** "The Lord shall establish thee an holy people unto himself, as he hath sworn unto thee, if thou shalt keep the commandments of the Lord thy God, and walk in his ways."

Verse 10: "And all people of the earth shall see that thou art called by the name of the Lord; and they shall be afraid of thee." **Verse 11:** "And the Lord shall make thee plenteous in goods, in the fruit of thy body, and in the fruit of thy cattle, and in the fruit of thy ground, in the land which the Lord sware unto thy fathers to give thee."

Verse 12: "The Lord shall open unto thee his good treasure, the heaven to give the rain unto thy land in his season, and to bless all the work of thine hand: and thou shalt lend unto many nations, and thou shalt not borrow." **Verse 13:** "And the Lord shall make thee the head, and not the tail; and thou shalt be above only, and thou shalt not be beneath; if that thou hearken unto the commandments of the Lord thy God, which I command thee this day, to observe and to do *them*:"

Verse 14: "And thou shalt not go aside from any of the words which I command thee this day, *to* the right hand, or *to* the left, to go after other gods to serve them."

Now, let's praise God together for His blessing in the reading of His word. This is a very unique formula in scripture that really works. There is a promise in this word of scripture when you obey. The rewards will have a lifetime effect on you to guarantee having a very abundant and prosperous life! Take the Bible as God speaking to you. It gives a clear picture of the outcome of your choices. You can either obey or do it your own way. Everything belongs to God. He has divine ownership over all!

Psalms 50: 10,12: "For every beast of the forest *is* mine, *and* all the cattle upon a thousand hills." **Verse 12:** "If I were hungry, I would not tell thee: for the world *is* mine, and the fulness thereof."

You see God knows where your prosperity is. He knows where the fish are and He'll show you how to get them. Establish in your heart that God is your source. He knows how to put you in the right place at the right time with the right people. You make the choice. Start with having fear, and reverencing our Master. You go in and possess with stewardship and honor. March forth as faithful stewards and servants. Honor the Lord with all of your substance. Don't hold back. Take God's right off the top immediately, regardless of anything else you may have to do. Pay now or pay later. You can reap the benefits now or suffer later. You make the decision; the choice is yours. Giving cheerfully gladdens the Lord's heart, and it shows no regrets, only belief. So, when you're faithful, the Lord promises:

St.Matthew 25: 23: "His lord said unto him, Well done, good and faithful servant; thou hast been faithful over a few things, I will make thee ruler over many things: enter thou into the joy of thy lord." Wow! What a beautiful promise from the Father, raising you to another level. That's what it is all about. However, you must pass your test. You must stand and not fall. If you fall, sincerely seek God's forgiveness. Get up, brush yourself off, and try it again.

Besides, it really saddens me that as Christians we can get so complacent, comfortable, and satisfied in our surroundings, living our lives this way from day to day not really being happy, yet we say that we are. However, if you can be totally honest with yourself to say that when you see others prospering, getting where you desire to be, getting things that you need and desire, that this doesn't bother you. Isn't there a longing to see what God can do for you? Don't misunderstand what I'm trying to say. I feel that we get too comfortable in a state of just getting by when the real reason is that we lack faith and courage to get there. Therefore, our faith is left shattered in a state of remission; being dormant.

Since our entire relationship with God is all based on faith, then what are we clinging to daily? You can't have active faith without it maturing.

When you water things, they grow. Don't stifle or choke out what God wants to raise up within you. We need to keep our faith active regarding things in our lives, always desiring to reach new levels in all things. To reiterate and to bring things on home and to bring back to your rememberance is: **Deuteronomy 8: 6-9,11,19: Verse 6:** "Therefore thou shalt keep the commandments of the Lord thy God, to walk in his ways, and to fear him." **Verse 7:** "For the Lord thy God bringeth thee into a good land, a land of brooks of water, of fountains and depths that spring out of valleys and hills;" **Verse 8:** "A land of wheat, and barley, and vines, and fig trees, and pomegranates; a land of oil olive, and honey;" **Verse 9:** "A land wherein thou shalt eat bread without scarceness, thou shalt not lack any *thing* in it; a land whose stones *are* iron, and out of whose hills thou mayest dig brass."

How sweet it is. It can't get any sweeter than that. If you've had any questions as to what God wanted of you, those were some of His requests. Adhere to them, and watch the blessings of the Lord flow richly into your lives. To continue in such abundance, do not forget who gives you all these things. As a reminder, there is **Verse 11:** "Beware that thou forget not the Lord thy God, in not keeping his commandments, and his judgments, and his statutes, which I command thee this day:" **Verse 19:** "And it shall be, if thou do at all forget the Lord thy God, and walk after other gods, and serve them, and worship them, I testify against you this day that ye shall surely perish."

When everything else fails, adhere to this method of hope and faith. The Lord says that with all He has, He loves each one of His children one by one, and name by name. He says that everything about "you" concerning "your" affairs is important to Him. In addition, do not be afraid; take hold of His hand to step out of the boat and onto the water. Fix your eyes upon Him and not on the circumstances surrounding you. Step out of your boat of comfort, and walk on the water. Come where there is rest, joy, peace, and happiness in your prosperous and abundant living.

Chapter XVI

Power To Get Wealth

Remember God gives you power to get wealth. So after everything has been said and done, you've achieved and accomplished all that you've set out to do. The ground that you walk upon, and everything surrounding you is blessed. *Do not forget the Lord!*

Deuteronomy 8: 12-18: "Lest *when* thou hast eaten and art full, and hast built goodly houses, and dwelt *therein;*"

Verse 13: "And *when* thy herds and thy flocks multiply, and thy silver and thy gold is multiplied, and all that thou hast is multiplied;"

Verse 14: "Then thine heart be lifted up, and thou forget the Lord thy God, which brought thee forth out of the land of Egypt, from the house of bondage;"

Verse 15: "Who led thee through that great and terrible wilderness, *wherein were* fiery serpents, and scorpions, and drought, where *there was* no water; who brought thee forth water out of the rock of flint;"

Verse 16: "Who fed thee in the wilderness with manna, which thy fathers knew not, that he might humble thee, and that he might prove thee, to do thee good at thy latter end;"

Verse 17: "And thou shall say in thine heart, My power and the might of *mine* hand hath gotten me this wealth."

Verse 18: "But thou shalt remember the Lord thy God: for *it is* he that giveth thee power to get wealth, that he may establish his covenant which he sware unto thy fathers, as *it is* this day."

I pray that this book on "*BANKRUPTCY – FILE WITH GOD NOT WITH MAN*" has been a great inspiration to those of you who have taken the time to read and ponder over every morsel and detail. It shall surely be a blessing to you and your soul. It's been so much of a blessing to me and an honor as well to share this wealth of information.

Through the writing of this book, I've received a much deeper revelation and meaning than ever before. I'm truly excited about the word of God and what it means for all of us. I can't think of anything else in this world with a much larger return than learning to "Trust In God!" It's wonderful having a God who's capable of watching over and protecting each and every one of us at all times. He knows how to make everything that's wrong—right! We have the very best and it doesn't get any better than that!

Chapter XVII

You Have The Victory

Psalms 34: 8: "O taste and see that the Lord *is* good: blessed *is* the man *that* trusteth in him." **Deuteronomy 8: 10:** "When thou hast eaten and art full, then thou shalt bless the Lord thy God for the good land which he hath given thee."

Look at God! He is so awesome in His own right that we are given an invitation to have our own personal experience regarding how good He really is. There is a promise made to you that says: if you trust in Him you will be blessed. God grants you the power and authority to eat of that good land. What an inspiring gift, and such a beautiful gesture. What intrigues me is the condition that follows after you've taken in as much as your heart desires and you are filled; the only request is that you *go and bless the Lord!* So, let's do it! The praises of God should be continually in your mouth and heart and it is time to triumph in victory over your successess.

Hallelujah! Glory to God in the highest! Oh, give thanks unto the Lord for He is good! Let us all raise our hands together and shout for joy. "For weeping may endure for a night but joy…I said joy…cometh in the morning." This is our morning!

I will sing…I will shout. I will praise His Holy name because I have won the Victory. I've won my long battle, and today I know that I am completely healed of the chains of bondage from my life—from my wallet—and all gridlocks which have been loosened by God this day. All that has been stolen from me by the devil, the Lord promises to multiply, and give it all back because the devil is a liar. "No weapon formed against me shall prosper." "Greater is He that's in me than he that is in the world," to paraphrase.

I Chronicles 29: 11: "Thine, O Lord, *is* the greatness, and the power, and the glory, and the victory, and the majesty: for all *that is* in the heaven and in the earth *is thine;* thine *is* the kingdom, O Lord, and thou art exalted as head above all." We must claim our inheritance this day for we are joint heirs of Christ! So stand to your feet right now, and leap for joy, saying with all of your heart: ***"I am an overcomer, an achiever, and I've conquered! For I have won the VICTORY, and the VICTORY is mine!"***

NOW YOU GO, and BLESS THE LORD!

Thank You For Saving My Life:
A Message From A Friend

The Spirit of the Lord spoke to me saying it is time to write a book on BANKRUPTY, "filing with God and not with man through a court of law" and to share my testimony with the world as to how He brought me out. I had no idea that people were going through and experiencing such things in this world as not being able to get a job because of filing bankruptcy. Did you know that Employers are now running credit reports on you as a part of the hiring process? Well I didn't but God did.

I was very shocked to say the least and appalled to hear that in this vast day and age this is going on. It seems as though dignity, honor and respect are becoming a rarity because of this unpleasant, unfortunate stigma.

Upon the completion of my book I began sharing the good news with friends, relatives, co-workers etc. In doing so the information given me has been the same from each person as their very own experience.

They have been placed in a position to fail because of not being fore-warned by the entities that encourage them to come on down and file these chapters. A very dear friend called on me just recently prior to my book going to print and asked me to pray for them regarding this same case scenario.

Although, their previous job held was for a very reputable company for over fifteen years and let go by way of reduction-in-force (layoff). I'd like to share their story first hand. It's a sad, desperate predicament and a plea for help. This is what they had to say:

"It is true what they say having a child changes your life. My son is the miracle that I asked God for and one of the best things that has ever happened to me. He has been hospitalized many, many times and put in ICU for his severe breathing problems since the age of eight months old.

"He is now eighteen years of age and I thank the Lord everyday for sparing his life. Because of the continuous doctor visits, non-stop medication and hospitalizations I eventually had to file bankruptcy. My son's health was always the number one priority in my life. Filing bankruptcy may take the creditors off of your back and stop your telephone from ringing off of the hook.

"However people begin to look at you differently and treat you differently. It is almost as if you are a criminal and they do not care about the reason as to what happened in your life to make such a decision. You become unworthy of anything that is normal for you to have such as, a new car, a nice place to live and even a good job.

"They say having bad credit speaks of your integrity and your character. They feel that because of this you may do something that is going to create unfavorable, undesirable or harmful results that will affect their company.

"Wow, doesn't the commitment to my son speak of my integrity, character and loyalty in being a good parent? Doesn't it show what a dedicated, devoted person I am who is trustworthy, reliable and will take full responsibility when there is an obligation to be met?

"Although our life is hard our faith has been made stronger than ever and I assure my son "that this to shall pass." He has turned out to be a wonderful young man who is very active in church. He has a heart of gold and this is a note that he wrote to the nurses at age eleven upon being released from the hospital."

> *"Thank you all so much for saving my life. You have sent me on the road to recovery. Because, you care I am still here. All your years of hard work have proven your excellence in this field. I am grateful, I am happy, I am still here.*
>
> *Thanks to you all another child will grow into society to be the best they can be. Your time and skills have secured the life of another patient.*
>
> *For all you have done I leave you these gifts to share amongst each other. You gave me another chance."*
>
> *"Thank you for saving my life."*

"We now just take it day by day and we pray a lot. Bad things do happen to good people and as far as filing bankruptcy sometimes there is no option and there will always be that cloud over your head so what do you do?"